SERIAL KILLERS BIG BOOK :

The Method and Madness of Monsters Pathways For Investigations

ROBERT J. MORTON

National Center for the Analysis of Violent Crime

stanfordpub.com

Contents

Message from the Director

Every day, law enforcement officers across America are called to respond to homicides. Each case is tragic. Each one means someone has lost a spouse, a parent, a sibling, or a child. Few cases, however, are more devastating and perplexing as serial murder.

These multiple victim crimes may span days, months, or even years, and can cross numerous jurisdictions. Often the relationship between suspect and victim is difficult to discern, and the motive may remain a mystery.

Investigators may have little to go on other than evidence at the crime scene where the murder victim is found. They face pressure from the public and the media to quickly solve these high-profile crimes, before the killer strikes again.

As the clock ticks, investigators with different levels of expertise must sift through a vast amount of information to narrow down their pool of suspects. Although much information has been published about serial killers, much of it may be of little use to investigators working an active serial murder investigation.

This monograph represents five years of empirical research gathered by experts at the FBI's National Center for the Analysis of Violent Crime. Our hope is that it will give our law enforcement partners the resources they need to better understand the motivations and behaviors behind these crimes, to discover the necessary correlations between potential suspects and cases, and to more expeditiously identify, arrest, and convict serial killers.

The FBI stands ready to assist our state, local, and international partners. We understand that the best way to combat any threat - be it terrorism, gang violence, or serial murder - is to combine our knowledge and resources with those of our partners, and to work as one team.

I appreciate the effort that went into this publication and would like to thank those who participated for their willingness to share their dedication, time and expertise. The report will be invaluable to our collective ability to understand, respond to, and prevent serial murder.

Robert S. Mueller, III

Acknowledgements

The NCAVC would like to gratefully acknowledge the contributions of the following individuals, without whose efforts this research project and monograph would not have been possible:

- Timothy R. Slater, Unit Chief, Behavioral Analysis Unit 2, for his unwavering support of this project.
- Yvonne Muirhead, Research Coordinator, NCAVC, for her continued support of this project.
- Special thanks go to Supervisory Special Agent Mark A. Hilts, FBI Behavioral Analysis Unit 3, who in his former capacity as the Unit Chief of Behavioral Analysis Unit 2, was unending in his support for this project for over 5 years. Without this support, publication of this document would not have been possible.
- Thanks to David A. Fletcher, FBI Training Division, for his contributions to the cover art.

Foreword

The Federal Bureau of Investigation's (FBI) National Center for the Analysis of Violent Crime (NCAVC) has traditionally been a frontrunner in the study of serial murder. The original 1980's study of serial and sexual murder conducted by NCAVC members was the catalyst for a plethora of research and study of serial murder by academicians, mental health practitioners and law enforcement professionals. The original and subsequent studies have analyzed serial murders from a number of perspectives, including historical reviews, individual case studies, descriptive projects, and causality factors.

Although a multitude of information has been published relating to serial murder, most of the studies were conducted from the perspective of an identified offender and concentrated on the offender's development; upbringing; familial relationships; history of physical, sexual, and emotional abuse; and other factors, which were viewed in terms of causality. A number of these studies, including the FBI's original study, also relied on self reported information obtained from offenders during interviews.

While developmental information concerning a serial killer provides interesting insights, it has little utility in helping identify an unknown offender during an active serial murder investigation for a number of reasons. First, this developmental information provides minimal assistance in highlighting potential suspects. Since individuals who are suspected of committing a crime do not usually divulge sensitive information concerning their childhood, especially regarding physical, emotional, or sexual abuse, these factors can remain hidden from an active law enforcement investigation. Second, there are significant legal restraints involved in gathering certain background information during an investigation, particularly those records that are safeguarded under privacy issues, such as medical and psychological records. This limits the amount of childhood history that is readily accessible. Third, it would be extremely time and manpower intensive for law enforcement personnel to obtain this information. Routinely, this information is gathered by conducting interviews of family members and acquaintances of the potential offender. This effort would be compounded in order to obtain the same information from multiple potential suspects. Fourth, even if investigators were able to acquire these records, the information would be of limited value. This is due to the wide range of factors involved in the upbringing and development of serial killers. All of these factors highlight the need for updated research material viewed through an investigative prism that is based upon information that would be available to law enforcement investigators working an active unsolved serial murder case.

In an effort to bridge this gap, the NCAVC undertook a new serial murder research project. For the past five years, this project gathered information from solved case files to construct a database containing serial murder cases, the offenders who commit them, and their unfortunate victims. This monograph is the culmination of that research project and provides a perspective of serial murder that originates with how the victim's body was disposed, a known factor in most murder investigations. This viewpoint will ultimately allow investigators to identify a number of situational factors based upon the particular body disposal scenario. Some of these factors include the approach an offender used to gain access to a given victim, the motivation involved in the crime, and the nature of the relationship between the offender and the victim. Further, it helps to discern certain offender characteristics that are identifiable during active investigations. The goal in publishing this monograph is to provide law enforcement investigators with relevant data that assists in the identification, arrest and conviction of serial murder offenders.

Additionally, the research data that is provided will offer a wide variety of pertinent information on serial murder in general. Included in this monograph are descriptive statistics and other measures that were utilized to gain a better understanding of the different types of offenders in this study. Lastly, this monograph will provide mental health practitioners, academicians, and law enforcement professionals with data that adds to the over-all body of knowledge concerning serial murder.

National Center for the Analysis of Violent Crime

The National Center for the Analysis of Violent Crime (NCAVC) is a component of the FBI's Critical Incident Response Group (CIRG), located at the FBI Academy in Quantico, Virginia. The primary mission of the NCAVC is to provide behaviorally-based, operational support to federal, state, local, and international law enforcement agencies involved in the investigation of unusual or repetitive violent crimes, communicated threats, terrorism, and other matters of interest to law enforcement. The NCAVC is comprised of five units: Behavioral Analysis Unit 1 (Counterterrorism and Counterintelligence), Behavioral Analysis Unit 2 (Threats, Cyber, White Collar Crime, and Public Corruption), Behavioral Analysis Unit 3 (Child Victims), Behavioral Analysis Unit 4, comprised of Adult Victims and the Violent Criminal Apprehension Program (ViCAP), and the Behavioral Research and Instruction Unit (BRIU).

NCAVC staff members conduct detailed analyses of crimes from behavioral, forensic, and investigative perspectives. The goal of this analysis process is to provide law enforcement agencies with a better understanding of the motivations and behaviors of offenders. The analysis is a tool that provides investigators with descriptive and behavioral characteristics of the most probable offender and advice regarding investigative techniques to help identify the offender.

The resources of the Behavioral Analysis Unit 4 (BAU-4) are focused on serial murders, sexual assaults, kidnappings, and other criminal acts targeting adult victims. BAU-4 members have developed significant expertise on the subject of serial murder and regularly provide operational assistance, conduct research, and provide training on issues related to serial murder.

The NCAVC also conducts research into violent crime from a law enforcement perspective. NCAVC research is designed to gain insight into criminal thought processes, motivations, and behaviors. Research findings are refined into innovative, investigative techniques that improve law enforcement's effectiveness against violent criminals and are shared with law enforcement and other disciplines through publications, presentations, and training.

Organization of Monograph

To make the information usable for investigators, this monograph is divided into a number of different sections. There are sections that provide law enforcement with an overview of serial murder investigations, as well as sections that address the implications of the various body disposal scenarios used by serial killers and discusses how this information can be used to highlight certain offender characteristics.

The study parameters and results section contains the statistical data of the study. The data was substantial enough to allow the authors to search frequencies and common occurrences between the body disposal scenario, other behaviors at the crime scene, the criminal history of the offender, and the relationship between the offender and the victim.

Included within these sections are comparisons between individual offenders based upon how many victims were killed by each serial killer. Age, marital status, pre-offense stressors, and arrest history were also compared between the offenders' first and last murder.

Additionally, a number of specific categories were isolated from the larger data set to provide information to law enforcement on these unique sets of serial murder. These categories include sexually motivated serial murders (Chapter VII); serial murders involving prostitutes (Chapter VIII); same sex serial murders (Chapter IX) and multiple motivations (Chapter X).

This monograph is not intended to provide a "profile" of serial murder offenders who fall into each pathway. However, this monograph is intended to provide guidance, insight, and knowledge concerning the behaviors and activities of these types of offenders.

I.

Introduction

Serial murder cases present numerous challenges and obstacles to law enforcement personnel who have the responsibility of investigating these complex cases. These cases involve multiple victims; the series may span days, months or even years; they can involve several jurisdictions; the motive involved may not be easily discerned; offender behaviors may not be consistent among all the cases; and there may be no obvious relationship between the offenders and the victims. Serial murder cases are also very rare and most law enforcement investigators do not have the same level of experience in investigating serial murder as they do with other types of crimes. Additionally, the majority of serial murder cases involve offenders who kill for sexual reasons. The crime scene dynamics in sexually motivated murders can appear very different from those of other violent crimes. The physical and particularly the sexual interactions committed by offenders against victims are unusual, tend to appear bizarre, and can be difficult to interpret (Morton & Hilts, 2008).

Typologies

There have been many attempts to classify serial murderers into distinct, inclusive typologies or categories. These classification systems sought to link certain personality types or behavioral patterns with different serial murder series. The typologies divided serial murderers into distinct categories based upon the offenders' behavior and perceived mental state at the time of the crime. Most of these studies utilized offender background and developmental information as well as interviews with offenders to determine this information. All of the studies were offered as templates to assist investigators working unsolved serial murders by providing personality characteristics of unknown offenders, based upon the typology.

One of the earliest attempts was the organized/disorganized classification developed by the FBI's Behavioral Science Unit (BSU) in the late 1980's (Ressler, Burgess, Douglas, Hartman & D'Agostino, 1986). It established two distinct dichotomous categories which were determined by an offender's behavior at a murder scene and were reflective of an offender's personality, development, criminal history, and social interactions. Generally, an organized offender was defined as an individual who planned his murders and displayed control at the crime scene. A disorganized offender was described as an individual who was spontaneous, their crime scenes appeared more muddled and the crimes were more opportunistic in nature. BSU held that organized offenders were more likely to plan a murder, utilize restraints, commit sexual acts on live victims, show or display control of a victim by manipulating or threatening, and use a vehicle during the commission of the murder. Disorganized offenders were more likely to leave weapons at the murder scene, pose the dead body, perform sexual acts on the dead body, keep a dead body, and not use a vehicle during the commission of the murder (Ressler et al., 1986).

The authors then applied this organized/disorganized typology to their research project, which involved interviews with 36 serial and sexual murderers who killed a total of 118 victims (Ressler et al., 1986). The organized/disorganized dichotomy was applied to these offenders to demonstrate its applicability. The results of this study have been widely reported and referenced. It has also been used extensively by criminologists, academicians and other researchers to explain serial murder dynamics.

Nevertheless the BSU members readily acknowledged that "...there are no situations where the organized and disorganized offenders are mutually exclusive" (Ressler et al., 1986, pp. 293). In an effort to acknowledge the diversity among offenders, in their 1992 book Crime Classification Manual, the authors created another category of offenders in which they entitled mixed. This category consisted of an offender who displayed characteristics from both the organized and disorganized categories (Douglas, Burgess, Burgess & Ressler, 1992). This third category simply indicates that serial offender behaviors are more accurately described as a continuum rather than a dichotomy.

Dichotomous typologies by their very nature have challenges, as an "either/or" choice, cannot possibly explain complex, multiple event human interactions. Therefore, this typology provides limited utility to law enforcement agencies investigating on-going serial murder cases given that most offenders display characteristics from both the organized and disorganized categories within this typology (Canter, Alison, Alison & Wentink, 2004).

Although BSU's earlier research into serial murder was ground breaking in its attempt to provide characteristics of serial murderers, there are serious short-comings with the research construction. The agents from the BSU traveled around the United States to conduct law enforcement training classes (Douglas & Olshaker, 1995). While at these training classes, they would identify convicted serial murderers in nearby prisons, who they contacted for an interview (Ressler et al., 1986). This approach created a sampling bias, an opportunity sample, which weakened the integrity of this study (Canter et al., 2004). The sample size of the study was small, consisting of only 36 murderers. This lessens the reliability of the results and diminishes any predictive value of the study. The study also depended on self-reported accounts from the murderers for a large portion of the information obtained. There are inherent limitations in utilizing this type of data, as some of the information cannot be validated independently.

Due to these limitations, applying the organized/disorganized dichotomy to active serial murder cases has limited utility in serial investigations. Further, the NCAVC has not embraced the organized/disorganized dichotomy for over 10 years and does not currently utilize the typology when reviewing cases in day to day operations.

The most widely used "motive" based categorical study is Ronald Holmes and James DeBurger's (1988) motivational model, which was also developed in the late 1980's. They identified four distinct motive types, and delineated them as visionary, mission-orientated, hedonistic and power/control oriented. The visionary type was described as killers who are classified as "psychotic". These killers receive commands from voices, or communicate with gods or other beings who demand the offender commit murder. Mission-orientated offenders kill to fulfill a need to "take charge" and to rid society of victims who they believe are burdens or are immoral. Hedonistic types kill to reinforce their quest for pleasure. They are divided into two subtypes, lust-orientated and thrill-orientated. Lust-orientated murderers are offenders who kill for sexual gratification. Thrill-orientated kill for their own excitement or thrills. Power/control orientated kill to exercise control and dominance over another human being.

Holmes and DeBurger (1988) stated they developed the individual category designations based upon "case information from solved cases as well as the characteristics of known offenders." Once the categories were identified, they used case examples that were specific to each of the individual categories to demonstrate the competence of their theory. In a subsequent work, Holmes and Holmes further delineated their categories, adding another category of the hedonistic type, described as comfort killers. These are offenders who kill for monetary gain (Holmes & Holmes, 2009).

There are many drawbacks to this type of categorical design. Once the case information was obtained, there was a lack of any empirical testing of the data (Canter & Wentink, 2004). Similar to the earlier FBI/BSU study, the source data was obtained through self-report information that was gathered from interviews with offenders. Further, the individual categories, again similar to the FBI BSU study, shared common characteristics across the typologies, making the determination of a single category difficult (Canter & Wentink, 2004).

In the late 1990's, Robert Keppel and Richard Walter adopted the rapist typologies originally devised by Groth et al. (1977) and converted them into homicide categories (Keppel & Walter, 1999). Groth et al. (1977), in their research concerning sexual assault, created four categories of rapists. They divided rapists into two general groupings, power rapists and anger rapists. They further divided the general groupings into four individual categories labeled power-reassurance, power-assertive, anger-retaliatory and anger-excitation.

According to Keppel and Walter (1977), the power-assertive rape-murder was planned as a rape but escalated to murder because the offender either wanted to increase his control of the victim, and/or the victim was killed to eliminate resistance by the victim, and/or to increase the offender's feeling of power. The power-reassurance rape murderer planned only the rape, but committed the murder when his "seduction" of the victim failed. The anger-retaliatory rape murderer planned both the rape and the murder. The murder allowed the offender to vent his anger by killing the victim, and providing him with revenge on a symbolic target. The anger-excitation rape murderer raped and killed the victim sadistically to gratify himself. In this category the rape and torture of the live victim were what satisfied the offender. Overall, the killing of the victim was just a necessity (Keppel & Walter, 1999).

In order to validate the use of the typologies put forth by Groth et al. (1977) as distinct murder categories, Keppel and Walter (1999) reviewed the circumstances of murder cases from a group of killers incarcerated in a state prison system. They then classified each individual murder and placed them into one of the individual categories, based upon the listed characteristics. According to Keppel and Walter (1999), this validated the use of the Groth et al. (1977) typologies as murder categories. However, no statistical measures were used to delineate between the categories, and none of the empirical characteristics were ever published (Keppel & Walter, 1999).

The reliability of applying this typology to serial murder is questionable. In the original research conducted by Groth et al. (1977), the typologies were based on the verbal, physical and sexual behavior of the offender. To obtain this information, the study utilized the reports of living rape victims, as well as interviews with offenders (Groth et al., 1977). These types of accounts would not be present in ongoing murder cases.

Additionally, in a number of published research studies on sexual homicide, it is well documented that the behavior in cases of sexual murder is distinctly different from the behavior in rape cases (Geberth, 1996). The primary difference is that in sexual murders, unlike sexual assault cases, the crime deliberately results in the death of the victim. Since the motivation for sexual murder is different from sexual assault, applying this typology without additional statistical measurement has little empirical integrity.

In summary, all of these studies have questionable reliability based upon their research construction. They are either based on a small sample size; have a lack of empirical testing across the typologies or categories; or the statistical measurements conducted were never published. Moreover, much of the information was obtained by self-report information provided directly by the offenders and not independently verified. Therefore the conclusions reached from these studies are arguably flawed and do not provide accurate information concerning the population of serial murderers.

The use of specific typologies or categories by law enforcement is difficult. Utilization of these different typologies requires investigators to analyze an offender's subtle behaviors and actions. They must then interpret those actions and use the results to classify the offender into one of these predetermined categories. Compounding this, the individual categories share numerous characteristics between them. Further, the behaviors needed to distinguish between the different categories may not be present. As a result, they provide minimal assistance to law enforcement working on-going serial murder cases since they are cumbersome to use, and therefore may not help to identify an unknown offender.

Myths

There are numerous myths regarding serial murder (Morton & Hilts, 2008). These have been propagated by movies, books, and television. The myths generally hold that all serial murderers are white males who are evil geniuses, and travel around the country killing multiple victims for sexual gratification. In addition, they state that serial killers are so cunning that they make purposeful mistakes that lead to their arrest because they secretly want to get caught by the police (Morton & Hilts, 2008).

There are also myths based upon the earlier serial murder research:

- All serial killers were raised in dysfunctional or abusive families.
- They are loners who are incapable of maintaining long term relationships.
- They increase in the violence they inflict on the victims as the series progresses.
- They attempt to engage the police in dialogue and learn about the progress of the investigation by frequenting police "hangouts."
- Once a killer starts murdering, he can never stop.
- If there is a time break in a series, the offender was either in prison, joined the military, went away to college, or was admitted to a mental health facility.

All of these myths greatly contribute to the inaccurate base of information concerning serial murder to the public in general and law enforcement specifically (Morton & Hilts, 2008).

Media Experts

The proliferation of so-called experts or "talking heads" further contributes to the myths of serial murder. The different media outlets routinely utilize retired law enforcement investigators, psychologists, academicians, and others to provide running commentary on ongoing, high profile criminal cases. These media experts are interviewed to discuss active serial murder investigations without having first-hand knowledge or details of the crimes. They also do not have information on the course of the particular investigation they are commenting about. Additionally, a number of them do not have any law enforcement investigative experience.

These instant assessments can be very detrimental to investigators working active serial murder cases because the erroneous information supplied can mislead potential witnesses or deter others from contacting the police with information about ongoing serial murder cases (Morton & Hilts, 2008). Additionally, it is well documented that a number of serial murderers actually follow the media in regards to their crimes. When these media experts make derogatory and misleading statements regarding a serial murderer, they also risk inflaming the murderer. Their comments may also interfere with a law enforcement strategy regarding media statements by providing contradictory information (Morton, & Hilts, 2008). Historically, comments by media experts provide little, if any, assistance to law enforcement attempting to capture a serial murderer.

Summary

The majority of previous research on serial murder has given minimal assistance to law enforcement working unsolved serial murder cases. Typologies and arbitrary categories that highlight subtle differences in serial offenders' mental state or developmental difficulties provide interesting perspectives; however, they provide minimal information that assists with the capture of an active, unknown serial murderer. These categories, coupled with the influence of the media, entertainment industry, and talking heads, have distorted the true nature of serial murderers.

This study, consistent with previous NCAVC efforts to assist investigators working serial murder cases, was embarked upon to provide investigators with information about serial murder that had a strong foundation in empirical findings regarding actual serial murder cases. More importantly, the focus of the study was to enhance investigative information for law enforcement investigators working active, unsolved serial murder cases.

II.

Study Parameters and Results

In order to provide law enforcement professionals with accurate information on serial murder, the authors conducted a research project based upon information, similar to what would be known in unsolved cases. The overarching focus of the project was to provide investigators with practical, empirically based information that would assist in the resolution of active serial investigations.

For purposes of this research study, the definition of serial murder is a single offender who killed at least two victims in separate events at different times.

This study utilized 480 cases of serial murder involving 92 offenders that were either submitted to the FBI's NCAVC by federal, state or local law enforcement agencies with requests for assistance, or solicited by the NCAVC for inclusion in the study. These cases span a 46 year time period, from 1960 to 2006, and occurred in the United States. Case files with missing or minimal information were excluded. Due to the nature of how these cases were obtained, it was not possible to obtain a representative sample of cases throughout the United States.

The cases selected for inclusion in this study were chosen based upon the following criteria:

- Each case involved a single offender who acted alone.
- The offender killed at least two victims in separate events, occurring at different times.
- The offender had either been found guilty during trial, plead guilty, accepted a guilty plea without admitting guilt, or there was a preponderance of evidence linking the offender to the specific offense or offenses.

The following factors concerning the offender, the victim, and the activity at the crime scene were examined:

- Motivation
- Victim selection and approach
- Method of killing
- Prior criminal history of the offender
- Demographic details of the offender and the victim
- Location where the victim was murdered
- Body disposal location
- Sexual activity, if any

Motivation was determined after a complete review of the case materials from the perspective of the "totality of circumstances." This broad view prevented a myopic view of the crime based on a single unusual factor. Although offenders may have multiple motivations for a single murder, this study utilized only the primary motivation.

The motives found in these cases were classified into the following categories:

- **Sexual** was defined as a murder motivated by sex. This included any type of sexual interaction, no matter how subtle or diverse. Since the basis for sexual interest varied according to the fantasies of the offenders, sexual penetration was not necessary for inclusion in the category.

- **Anger** was defined as a motivation in which an offender killed victims based on personal pent-up hostility which was projected towards a person or group represented by the victim. The victim could have been a symbol of this hostility, or may have just been an available, vulnerable target to the offender. Included within this category were also cases where the offender was jealous or seeking revenge.
- **Mental illness**, although not technically a motivation, this "motive" was utilized as a category to cover the cases in which an offender appeared to demonstrate symptoms of various psychiatric maladies. In turn, those symptoms were a significantly contributing factor for the murders. There were some cases in which offenders were clinically diagnosed by mental health professionals; however, the majority of the included cases were based upon third party reporting of obvious psychiatric features.
- **Profit** was defined as the killing of victims in order for the offender to profit financially from the death of the victims.
- **Other** category was utilized to capture any other motivation not previously described.

The primary means an offender used to approach and gain access to the victims were as follows:

- **Ruse** was defined as a trick or con to gain access to the victim.
- **Blitz** was defined as an immediate physical attack, without any verbal interaction.
- **Surprise** was defined as a situation where the offender utilized stealth, and capitalized on circumstances, locations, or timing to confront the victim.

The relationship between the offender and the victim were described as:

- **Stranger** was defined as no known relationship between the offender and the victim.
- **Targeted stranger** was defined as a situation where the offender knew who the victim was, but the victim had no knowledge or familiarity with the offender.
- **Acquaintance** was defined as a relationship involving prior contact between the offender and the victim however slight. This could range from situations where the offender and the victim lived in the same neighborhood and had casual contact; to relationship situations where both the offender and the victim were well acquainted with each other.
- **The relative/familial** category included blood relatives as well as blended family and extended family relationships.
- **Customer/client** was a distinct category and involved situations where the victim was a prostitute and the offender was posing as the customer.

The categories utilized for body disposal were framed within two distinct contexts in which bodies were transported from the murder scene and left at the murder scene.

- A body transported from the murder scene was further categorized as **dumped** or **concealed**.
  - **Dumped** was defined as the offender depositing the victim's body with no apparent concern that the victim would be discovered. Dumped bodies were usually left in public places.

- **Concealed** was defined as the offender hiding or concealing the victim's body for a number of reasons. This was to either delay discovery of the victim's body; to destroy physical evidence; or to use time to distance the discovery of the victim's body from any observable contact between the offender and the victim. This also included placing the bodies of the victims in isolated locations that delayed discovery of the victims.
    - There were three separate scenarios utilized under the concealment category: **left in a body of water, left on the surface of the ground,** or **buried in a clandestine grave**.

- A body that was left at the murder site was further categorized as either left "**as is**" or **concealed**.
    - Left "**as is**" was defined as the body disposal scenario where the offender made contact with the victim within the victim's residence or took a victim into an abandoned building, killed the victim, and afterward left the victim inside that same structure.
    - Additionally, bodies that were **displayed** were included within the category left "**as is**" due to the small number of cases. **Displayed** was defined as the offender intentionally positioning the victim's body after death to shock the police, the victim's family, or the general public; or to provide a message concerning the offender's opinion of the victim or class of victims.
    - **Concealed** was defined as hiding or concealing the victim's body to delay discovery for a number of reasons. This was to either delay discovery of the victim's body; to destroy physical evidence; or to use time to distance the discovery of the victim's body from any observable contact between the offender and the victim. This also included placing the bodies of the victims in isolated locations that delayed discovery of the victims.

The state of dress of the victims was identified as fully dressed, nude, partially nude, or redressed.

The causes of death were taken verbatim from the autopsy reports, and contributing traumas were also included. The authors had access to extensive case material and on occasion offender interviews. Information regarding locations and the cause of death was able to be determined for the majority of the victims whose bodies were partially or never recovered. Criminal history information was obtained from the offender's NCIC record.

Demographics of both the offender and the victim that were captured were gross descriptors such as gender, race, age at time of murder, educational background, employment or occupation history, marital status at the time of the murders, and psychiatric history. Additionally, all of the offenders were male. Serial murder is a low base rate phenomenon that rarely occurs in society and even more infrequently involves a female offender. Due to the lack of submitted cases to the NCAVC, this study did not include female offenders. The lack of female participants in the study may present a slightly skewed image of serial murderers.

To obtain information regarding the above-listed criteria, a comprehensive review of the entire case file was conducted. This process included a review of:

- Police investigative reports
- Crime scene reports and photographs
- Autopsy reports and photographs
- Results of any forensic testing
- Background information regarding the victim
- Background information concerning the offender

Background information on offenders was purposely limited to gross descriptors and previous arrest records, to highlight the information that would be readily available to investigators prior to identification of a specific offender.

After the complete case file was reviewed by the authors, the collection instrument was completed. The collection instrument and case file were then reviewed jointly by at least two of the authors for consensus. The results of the collection instruments were entered into IBM SPSS version 20.0 (IBM SPSS Inc., Chicago, IL) for data analysis.

In general, descriptive statistics provide an overall picture of the composition of the entire data set. This information includes the demographics of the offenders and the victims, education, military history, employment history, and arrest records.

Victims

The victims were primarily female (75.4%) and ages ranged from 8 to 91 years:

- 8 to 13 years (3.3%)
- 14 and 29 years (50.4%)
- 30 to 45 years (29.4%)
- 46 to 60 years (6.7%)
- Over 60 years (7.6%)
- Unknown (3.3%)

The racial breakdown for victims:

- White (60.2%)
- Black (29.8%)
- Other (10.0%)

The racial breakdown for victims of serial murder has more White victims than Black victims and is in contrast to the reported numbers of murders per year where almost the same number of whites and blacks are killed each year (U.S. Department of Justice, 2010).

Offenders

In this study's data set, all of the offenders were male. The racial breakdown for offenders is as follows:

- White (52.2%)
- Black (38.0%)
- Hispanic (7.6%)
- Other (2.2%)

Offenders ages ranged from 15 to 45 years at the time of the first murder, to 18 to 60 years of age at the time of their last murder. The majority of offenders were in the age group of 15 to 45 years of age (94.6%), with the largest number of offenders falling in the 27 to 37 years of age category (52.2%).

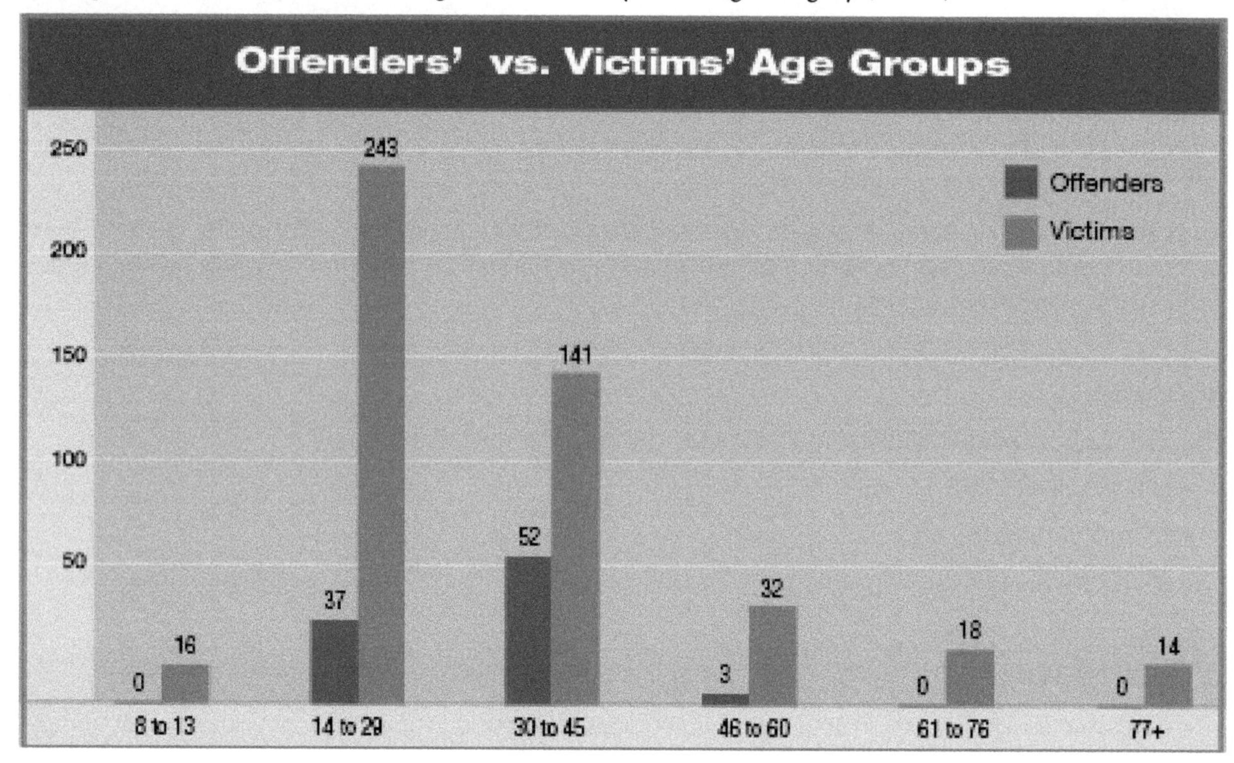

The average educational level for offenders was a high school diploma or further education (70.2%), with 39.0% of those offenders having education beyond high school. At the time of their arrest, 30.4% of offenders were married. Over one third of offenders (34.8%) had served in the United States military.

The high education level reflects the intelligence level of these offenders.

A large percentage of offenders had arrest records; however, 78.3% had a record at the time of their first murder versus 88.0% that had a record at the time of last murder. The majority of the arrests were for misdemeanors, and the specific offenses that offenders were arrested for were spread across 20 different offenses or classes of offenses. At the time of arrest, the leading categories of offenses:

- Assault/battery offenses (12.9%)
- Theft/larceny offenses (10.6%)
- Sex related offenses (9.0%)
- Burglary (8.0%)
- Drug offenses (6.2%)

A total of 21.7% of offenders did not have any arrest record at the time they committed their first murder.

Arrest Frequencies

Crime	First Murder		Last Murder	
	n	Percent	n	Percent
Arson	7	2.2%	7	1.8%
Assault	42	13.0%	50	12.9%
Burglary	28	8.7%	31	8.0%
Disorderly Conduct	9	2.8%	10	2.6%
Drug/Narcotics	16	5.0%	24	6.2%
DUI/DWI	7	2.2%	8	2.1%
Homicide	5	1.5%	11	2.8%
Kidnapping/Abduction	9	2.8%	12	3.1%
Motor Vehicle Theft	14	4.3%	18	4.6%
Prostitution/Solicitation	3	0.9%	3	0.8%
Robbery	15	4.6%	19	4.9%
Sex Offenses	31	9.6%	35	9.0%
Theft/Larceny	38	11.8%	41	10.6%
Stolen Property	6	1.9%	8	2.1%
Trespass	17	5.3%	18	4.6%
Vandalism	7	2.2%	7	1.8%
Weapon Law Offenses	19	5.9%	23	5.9%
Fraud	7	2.2%	10	2.6%
Violation of Probation/Parole	11	3.4%	15	3.9%
Violation of Restraining Order	1	0.3%	1	0.3%
Other	31	9.6%	37	9.5%
Total	**323**	**100.0%**	**388**	**100.0%**

Previous studies on serial murder had higher rates of burglary and sex related offenses (Keppel & Walter, 1999; Chan & Heide, 2009).

Prior to arrest, 32.6% of offenders were formally diagnosed by a mental health professional with a psychiatric disorder. The diagnoses of these offenders:

- Personality disorder (42.9%)
- Psychotic disorder (19.0%)
- Developmental disorders (11.9%)
- Mood disorders (11.9%)

The rate of diagnosed psychiatric disorders (32.6%) is higher than the rates quoted for the general population (21.0% to 25.0%) (Center for Disease Control, 2004; U.S. Surgeon's General Report, 1999).

A majority of these offenders (73.9%) also had some type of stressor at some time either prior to their murders or during their series of murders. These were very diversified, with alcohol or drug abuse (23.9%) and legal difficulties (16.7%), being the most prevalent.

Offender/Victim Relationships

The relationships between the offenders and the victims were:

- Customer/client (41.5%)
- Strangers (31.5%)
- Acquaintances (12.1%)
- Targeted strangers (11.7%)
- Unknown (1.9%)

Customer/client was developed because of the number of murders that involved victims who were engaging in prostitution.

The primary approaches utilized by offenders were:

- Ruse/con (65.4%)
- Surprise (16.9%)
- Blitz (5.0%)
- Unknown (12.5%)

The majority of offenders (90.2%) and victims (90.0%) were either White or Black. However, White offenders (52.2%) killed 55.0% of all victims. Black offenders (35.4%) killed 35.5% of the victims.

Race distribution of serial offenders and their victims

Victim Race (n=480)	Offender Race		
	White	Black	Other**
White (n=289)	37.5%	16.0%	6.6%
Black (n=143)	10.8%	17.9%	1.0%
Other* (n=46)	6.4%	1.4%	1.6%
Unknown (n=2)	0.4%	-	-

*Other victim races include Hispanic, Asian and Native American.
**Other offender races include Hispanic and Asian.

Number of Murders

The number of murders that were committed in the series varied from 2 to 23 victims:

- Two to four victims (60.9%)
- Five to nine victims (27.2%)
- Ten or more (12.0%)

Of the thirty six offenders (39.1%) who killed five or more victims, twenty two were White and eleven were Black, killing a total of 191 and 148 victims, respectively.

Due to the prolific nature of the serial offenders in this study, those who killed three or more victims account for 91.6% of the victims.

Time Frames

The time frame was calculated between when the murders occurred and when the victims' bodies were recovered.

- Victims found less than one day after murder (34.2%)
- Victims found between one and fifteen days (29.6%)
- Victims found after fifteen days (12.1%)

Since a majority of victims are found in a relatively short time, proper evidence processing and collection may lead to identifiable forensic evidence linking a serial offender to a number of murders.

The offenders' time span between murders was determined from the date of the first murder to the date of the last murder or date of last known contact. The time span for the murder series was able to be calculated for the majority of offenders (91.3%, n=84). Most of the serial murder series occurred within a nine year time span (86.0%, n=73). The remaining offenders' (13.1%, n=11) murder series lasted longer than ten years with two offenders series lasting over 20 years. For the majority of these offenders, the interruptions in their series were due to the fact that normal life activities took up greater portions of their time (Morton & Hilts, 2008).

In order to examine offenders behavior across the time sequence of their offenses, certain crime features and offender descriptive statistics were viewed between the time of their first and last murders. There were a few crime characteristics which showed no variability:

- Level of violence showed little to no escalation
- Number of sex acts remained fairly constant

Within this study population, serial offenders' behavior was consistent from crime to crime and there was little to no escalation in violence.

Analysis of the data revealed few differences in the offender characteristics at the time of the first murder compared to the last murder. For example, more offenders were married at the time of their last murder (30.4%) compared to the first murder (25.0%). Additionally, they had more formal education and more arrests.

This data contradicts earlier studies of serial murder that described offenders as being loners and incapable of maintaining a long term relationship (Ressler et al., 1986; Douglas & Olshaker, 1995; Meloy, 2000).

Interstate versus Intrastate

Serial killers usually kill within a defined comfort zone of their choosing. Most of the murders were committed intrastate (72.3%), with 26.9% committed interstate. The offenders who operated interstate either lived in areas that were adjacent to state borders, were geographically close; were employed in occupations that allowed state to state travel (i.e. long haul truck drivers); or they were transitory in their lifestyles and moved from area to area.

Myth: All serial murderers travel state to state to kill victims. The findings from this study debunk this myth.

Motivation

The motivations for the murders were:

- Sex (81.5%)
- Profit (5.0%)
- Anger (3.1%)
- Mental illness (1.3%)
- Other (5.6%)
- Unknown (3.5%)

Other motivations included witness elimination and murder for hire.

The majority of the cases in this study were sexually motivated; however, this only reflects the cases that were referred to the NCAVC for analysis. There are also a number of other types of serial murder that are rarely referred to the NCAVC. These include health care serial killers and organized crime or drug "hit men". These types of cases were not included in this study.

A review of the literature on serial murder reveals that most of the serial murder cases investigated by law enforcement are sexually motivated (Chan & Heide, 2009; Meloy, 2000).

Causes of Death (COD)

Primary causes of death were:

- Strangulation (42.5%) includes manual and ligature strangulation, suffocation, and asphyxia
- Blunt force trauma (BFT) (16.3%)
- Stab wounds (12.9%)
- Gunshot wounds (GSW) (12.9%)
- Undetermined (6.3%)
- Other (2.9%)

Other causes of death include drowning, drugs, and poisoning.

In 36.9% of the cases, the offender brought a weapon to commit the murder.

The most common causes of death reflect the intimate nature of the studied serial offenders who preferred to kill by means that bring them into close contact with their victims.

Sexual Contact

There was evidence that 72 offenders (78.1%) committed 350 sex acts on 226 victims (see Table A.2). DNA was recovered in 22.7% of the cases and victims were found nude or partially nude in 64.5% of the cases. Bindings were utilized in 29.0% of the cases. There were a few cases of unusual crime scene behaviors. In fifteen cases the body cavities/genitalia of the victims were mutilated, bite marks were evident in nine cases, six cases of evisceration, three cases of cannibalism, three cases of carving/writing and two cases where the victims were skinned. There was also evidence of post-mortem mutilation in 12.1% of the cases and post mortem sex in 15.0% of the cases.

The low incidents of unusual crime scene behaviors is in contrast to earlier studies that showed higher instances of this type of behavior (Ressler et al., 1986; Canter, Alison, and Wentink, 2004).

Race distribution of serial offenders and committed sexual acts

Sexual Acts (n=350)	Offender Race			
	White (n=34)	Black (n=30)	Other* (n=8)	Total
Vaginal Sex	71(21)	60(27)	18(7)	149
Anal Sex	46(20)	35(17)	2(1)	83
Oral Sex on Offender	34(14)	16(9)	5(4)	55
Oral Sex on Victim	17(6)	-	-	17
Fondling	18(6)	-	1(1)	19
Masturbation	15(4)	2(1)	-	17
Foreign Object Penetration	4(3)	4(3)	-	8
Digital Penetration	1(1)	-	1(1)	2
Total	206	117	27	350

Note. Numbers in parentheses represent total number of offenders who committed sex acts. Some offenders committed multiple acts on the same victim.
**Other race includes Hispanic and Asian.*

Sites/Locations

The different sites or locations involved in each of the murders were described as the initial contact, the assault, the murder, and the disposal site. The locations were not mutually exclusive and in some of the cases, all of the events occurred in the same location.

A review of the case information revealed that most of the offenders had knowledge of and familiarity with all of the locations in the murder sequence.

The sites where offenders initially had contact with victims:

- Known vice areas (30.8%)
- Outdoor public areas (24.2%)
- Victims' residences (22.7%)
- Indoor locations in public areas (10.8%)

More White offenders (28.3%) had their initial contact with victims in an outdoor area as compared to Black offenders (13.0%). More Black offenders (17.4%) had contact with a victim in a known vice area compared to White offenders (15.2%).

The assault sites:

- Outdoor public areas (22.3%)
- Victims' residences (21.9%)
- Offenders' residences (18.3%)
- Offenders' vehicles (14.0%)

The murder sites:

- Outdoor public areas (25.8%)
- Victims' residences (22.1%)
- Offenders' residences (18.1%)
- Murder location was not identified (13.5%)
- Offenders' vehicles (11.5%)

The locations where the victims' bodies were disposed:

- Outdoor public areas (61.5%)
- Victims' residences (20.8%)
- Interior locations in public areas (5.8%)
- Other living quarters (4.8%)
- Offenders' residences (3.8%)

The authors had access to extensive case material and on occasion offender interviews. Information regarding locations and the cause of death was able to be determined for the majority of the victims, even those whose bodies were partially or never recovered. Victims' bodies were not fully recovered in 27 cases (5.6%). In eleven cases, partial body parts (skull/head, torso) were found. Additionally, victims' bodies were found in bags (3.8%), wrapped in bedding/tarps (3.5%), containers (3.3%), vehicles (1.5%), and dumpsters (1.3%).

Only seven victims (1.5%) were displayed at the crime scene which is in contrast to other studies of serial murder that reported much higher frequencies of this behavior (Ressler et al., 1986; Douglas & Olshaker, 1995; Chan & Heide, 2009).

Evidence Tampering

Evidence was destroyed or removed from crime scenes in 36.3% of the cases. In addition, the crime scene was cleaned in 15.2% of the cases. In nearly half of the cases (44.6%), offenders took no actions to alter the crime scene. Similarly, in 58.5% of the cases, offenders took no precautions to disguise their identity or avoid leaving physical evidence. In 8.8% of the cases, the offender wore gloves and in 2.7% of the cases, he wore a condom.

In over half of the cases (54.0%), offenders removed multiple items from the crime scene. Of those cases (n=259), the majority of items taken were:

- Clothing or shoes (48.5%)
- Jewelry (31.7%)
- Wallet or purse (23.6%)
- Money (20.5%)

There have been many references throughout the literature published on serial murder identifying items that serial murderers take from crime scenes as trophies or souvenirs. There were multiple explanations as to the meaning of this behavior. In this study; however, we only identified the items taken and did not interpret any intrinsic meaning.

III.

Serial Murder Investigations

Active, ongoing serial murder investigations present many different challenges to law enforcement. These vary from the external pressure exerted by the public, the media, and law enforcement management, to the frustration felt by the line investigators who can't identify the offender. In the majority of serial murder cases, there is no identifiable relationship between the offender and the victims. This differs from most violent crime investigations where there is a recognizable connection between the offender and the victim. This lack of a relationship between the offender and the victim precludes routine police investigation where the investigation begins with the victim and their known relationships with spouses, sexual partners, friends, acquaintances, business partners, and rivals. Instead, the factors that link the cases are the offender and the choices he makes in the commission of his murders.

Crime Scene Assessment

Analysis begins with the crime scene, as the interaction between the offender and the victim can highlight a number of factors:

- The approach to the victim
- The nature of the physical interaction
- The nature of the sexual interaction (if any)
- Choice of weapon or weapons
- The manner of death
- Method of body disposal

All these factors can also help determine the criminal experience and skill of the offender.

Victimology

Along with victim/offender interaction, the victims' risk factors are another key element in investigating serial homicides. The victims' risk levels can be defined as the degree to which the individuals' personality, behavior, lifestyle, habits, physical attributes, location, circumstances, judgment, security consciousness and/or other personal factors affected the probability of criminal victimization. Victims' risk levels are determined using victimology information, which includes:

- Gender
- Age
- Occupation
- Marital status
- Former intimate relationships
- Prior arrest history
- Drug and/or alcohol use or abuse
- Type of residence
- Neighborhood dynamics
- Community crime rate

Victims can be classified on a continuum anywhere from low to high risk. A low risk victim is a person who generally has a minimal probability of criminal victimization. A moderate risk victim is a person who generally has a minimal probability of criminal victimization but due to behavior, atypical or otherwise, the risk was situationally elevated at the time of victimization. A high risk victim is a person who generally has a high probability of criminal victimization.

Victimology information can help identify how an offender is choosing victims. Offenders chose victims based upon three criteria.

- **Availability**: Offenders access to victims.
- **Vulnerability**: The situations and circumstances in victims' lives that allow offenders to victimize them.
- **Desirability**: The attractiveness viewed in potential victims (sexual murders) or the choice of victims by offenders for other intrinsic needs.

Utilizing the crime scene analysis together with the victimology information can reveal if offenders were targeting particular victims or finding victims of opportunity within a hunting area. Hunting areas are described as geographic areas offenders identify, become familiar with, and then later utilize to attack potential victims that enter into those locations.

Motivation

Motivation is determined by examining a combination of elements, including the victim/offender interaction, choice of victim, and forensic evidence. Although killers who share motivations may have a number of similar traits, the specific factors or the combination of these factors differ from killer to killer. The reason for the differences lay within the unique confluence of the individual killer, the choice of victims, the means of killing, and the proclivities of the killer. Proper analysis of motivation requires investigators to examine all of these factors.

Case Linkage

Case linkage of different murders is central to identifying a serial killer. It is paramount to identify the first murder or attempted murder in a series. Similar to other human behavior, the first time an event is performed, the greater the chances for mistakes to be made. These errors can assist in the identification of an unknown offender.

Case linkage is based upon the following factors:

- Consistent Method of Operation (M.O.)
- Similar choices of victims
- Common approaches to victims
- Similar physical and/or sexual interactions
- Use of similar weapons

- Similar causes of death
- Forensic results
- Geographic locations of murders
- Temporal aspects including time of day, day of week, and time of year

Investigations

Searching for a serial killer requires investigators to view the investigation as a summary of the following elements.

- **Geographic**: Is the area the serial killer is operating in a rural, suburban or inner city environment? Does the offenders' choices of victims limit where potential victims are located? Additionally, is the area predominately inhabited by a single racial group or is the area racially mixed? This can indicate the race of the offender as it can show the offender's ability to move freely throughout a community without being noticed.

- **Type of victim**: Is the offender targeting specific victims or utilizing a "hunting area" and targeting any potential victim that enters the area? Are there other factors that the offender is specifically targeting (e.g. prostitutes)?

- **Means of accessing victims**: How does the offender come in contact with the victims? Is the offender entering a residence to attack victims, picking up a prostitute on the street, or utilizing other circumstances? Each of these scenarios require the offenders to have different abilities and experiences.

- **Use of weapons or manner of death**: Does the offender's choice of a weapon highlight any prior experiences? Does the manner of death also highlight previous experiences? Is the offender competent with the weapon or manner of death? All of these factors can reveal if the offender has certain background characteristics.

- **Interactions with the victim**: Do the physical or sexual interactions with the victims reveal any proclivity or previous experience? Certain distinct behaviors may indicate the offender has committed other types of crimes.

- **Body disposal location/manner**: The choice of a particular body disposal location may reflect the offender's familiarity with the area. The manner of the body disposal can also reflect the nature of the relationship between the offender and the victim.

Since the body disposal scenarios reveal different crime characteristics and ultimately different offender characteristics, the manner of body disposal is one of the central factors to case solution.

The key to identifying potential suspect pools originates with correctly identifying the dynamics involved in a serial murder case. These dynamics consist of a collation of different factors:

- Method of Operation (M.O.)
- Forensics

- Offender/victim interaction
- Motivation
- Victim selection
- Victim targeting area
- Victimology

Practically, the biggest issue facing investigators deals with the mechanics of sorting through the vast amount of information generated in these types of investigations and the means to identify the serial killer within the many different potential pools of suspects. These potential suspect pools are the key to successfully identifying a serial killer.

As in other human interactions, there are unique elements attributable to each individual. As a result, each of the offenders' subsequent behaviors during violent interactions may have some unique features. All of these factors need to be identified and considered. The idea is to utilize the elements identified in a particular serial murder as a source of potential suspect pools. By dividing these elements into lists, and then cross-checking the various lists, potential suspects can be highlighted. The elements do not create a checklist in which investigators simply plug one or two factors into a template and that template reveals a single offender. Instead, they provide measures of certain behaviors of offenders based upon a confluence of elements that result in a pool or several pools of potential suspects.

The majority of investigators do not have the same experience level with serial murder investigations as they do in other types of crime. Subject matter experts can be highly beneficial in assisting the investigative agency with unusual intricacies involved in these types of cases. The FBI's National Center for the Analysis of Violent Crime is uniquely qualified to provide investigative and behavioral assistance, case linkage, profiles of unknown offenders, media strategy, interview strategy, and prosecutive assistance.

IV.

Body Disposal Pathways

The goal of this research is to use the information from the different body disposal scenarios to highlight potential serial offenders within the suspect pool in active serial murder investigations. The reasoning for this is founded in a number of factors:

- The body disposal site is usually the initial scene law enforcement professionals are exposed to in their investigation.
- The manner and circumstances of the body disposal can lead to logical conclusions concerning the nature of the crime.
- The different body disposal scenarios reflect varied criminal experience levels of offenders.
- The manner of body disposal may show a potential relationship between the offender and the victim.

The different body disposal scenarios used by offenders were separated into four distinct body disposal pathways described as: Transported from the Murder Site and Concealed; Transported from the Murder Site and Dumped; Left "As Is" at the Murder Site; and Left at the Murder Site and Concealed.

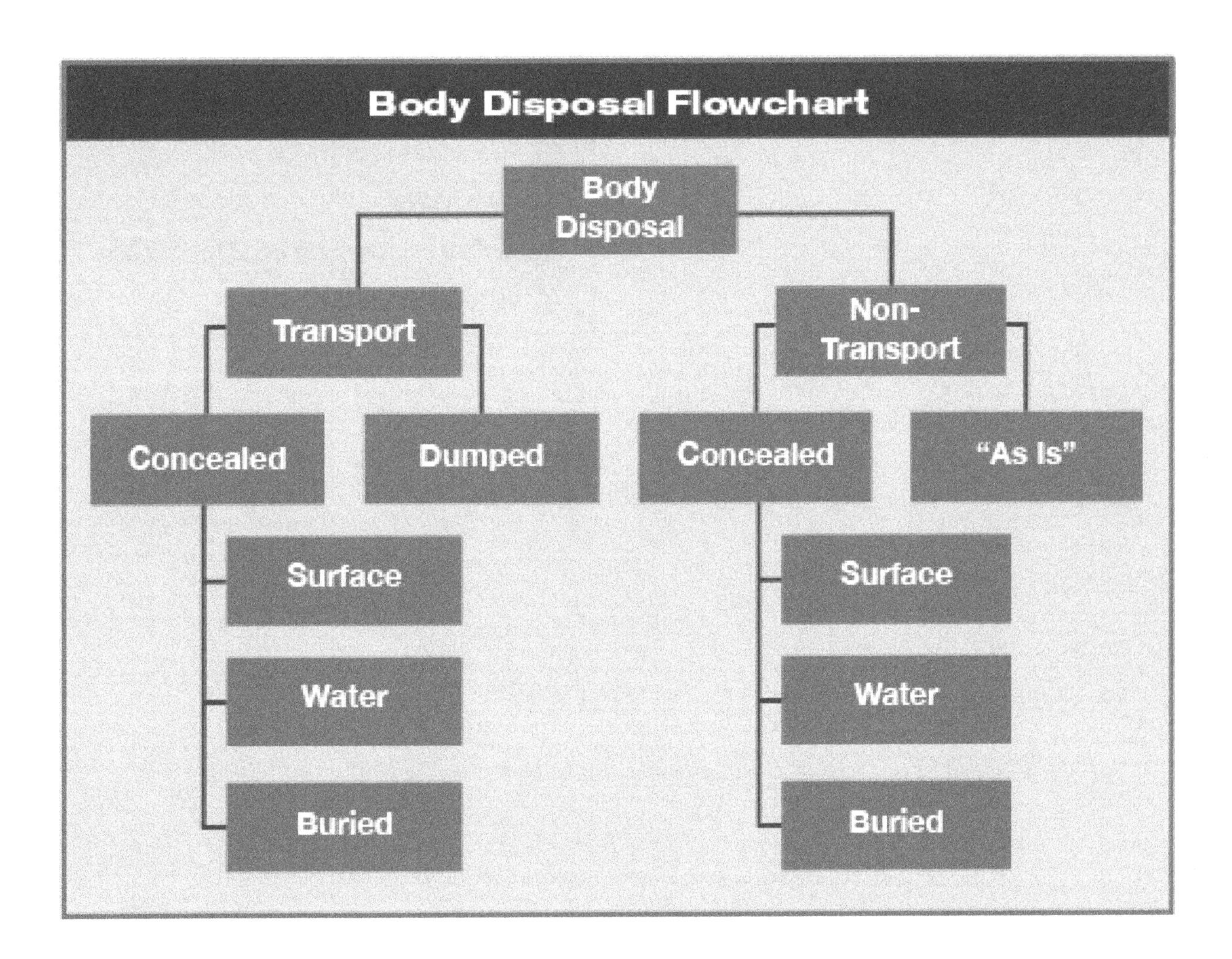

The authors then determined which offenders (n = 42 offenders; n = 166 victims) consistently utilized the same pathway throughout the duration of their murder series and which offenders (n = 48 offenders; n = 293 victims) changed pathways between victims. Of note, investigators were unable to recover victims' bodies for the two remaining offenders and therefore could not determine a particular pathway (n = 2 offenders; n = 21 victims, 19 victims were never recovered).

Both sets of offenders were further analyzed. Results concerning offenders who used the same pathway for all their murders are found in Chapter V. Results for offenders who did not use the same pathway are found in Chapter VI.

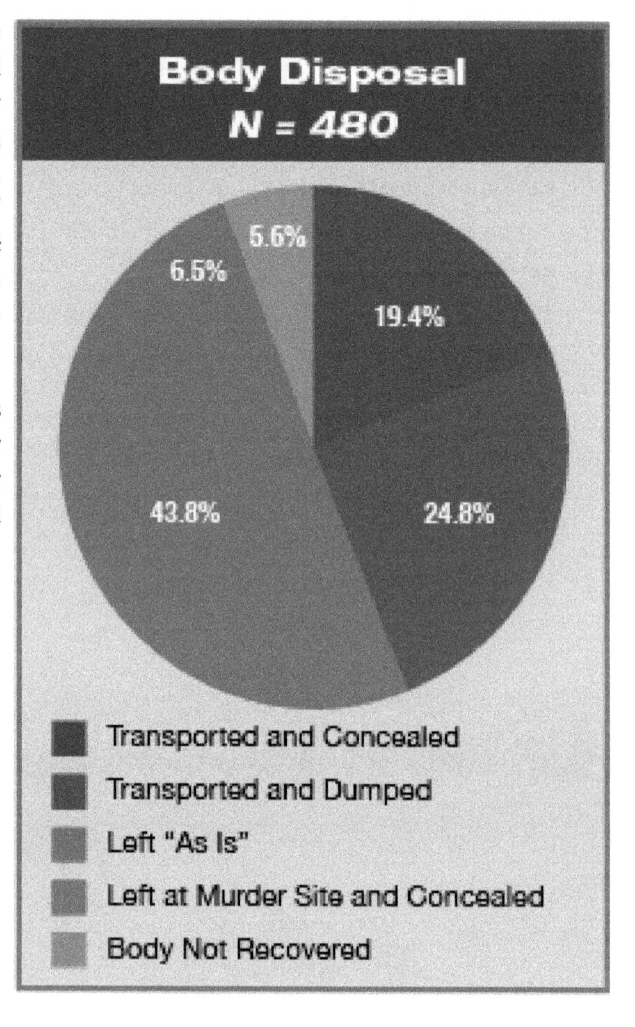

V.
Offenders Who Used Same Body Disposal Scenarios

Characteristics of the offenders (n=42) and their victims (n=166) that were unique to each pathway are provided below.

Pathway #1: Transported from the Murder Site and Concealed

A total of 10 offenders utilized this pathway murdering 31 victims. In examining the locations where victims were concealed:

- Surface: Total of 15 victims
- Water: Total of 9 victims
- Buried: Total of 7 victims

These cases occurred when the victims' bodies were transported from the murder sites to separate disposal sites and the bodies were concealed or hidden from view. The movement of the victims' bodies by offenders increases the chances that an offender may be seen or identified in the vicinity of the murder site and/or disposal site. This movement is extremely risky for an offender, yet these offenders are compelled to move the victims. There are two main reasons offenders concealed victims' bodies:

- To delay or prevent discovery
- In order to place time and distance between themselves and the victims

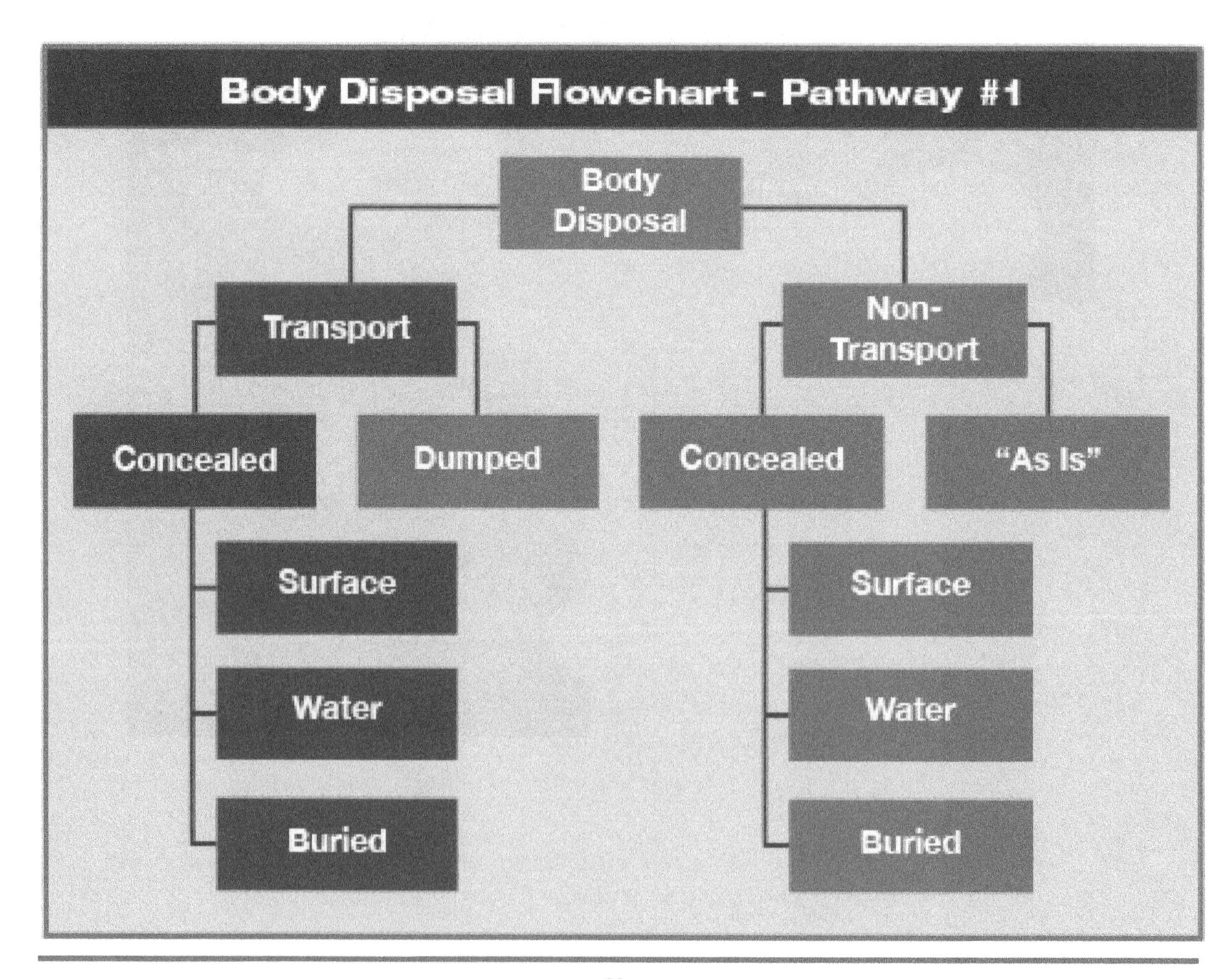

Why? Because offenders perceive that law enforcement will recognize some connection that will link them to the victim. Also, some serial killers do not want law enforcement or the general public to know that they are actively killing victims. Attention by the media highlighting that a serial killer is operating will often make it more difficult for the offender to find more victims.

Frequent Occurrences within Pathway #1

Offenders

- All were White.
- Offenders were between the ages of 24-43 and six of the ten offenders were not married.
- 90.0% were working full-time at the time of the murder.
- Over half had an education beyond high school.
- Half had prior military service.
- 40.0% had a diagnosed psychiatric disorder prior to the murder.
- All of the offenders had a criminal history; however, no offenders had arrests for patronizing prostitutes.
- Almost 80% of offenders killed between two and four victims.

Victims

- Majority were White.
- Most victims were between 11 and 29 years of age.
- All victims were female.
- Ten of the victims were prostitutes and the offenders had initial contact with them in known vice areas.
- In 61.3% of the cases, the offender was a stranger to the victim.

Crime Scene

- The majority of offenders utilized a ruse/con approach to gain access to the victims.
- In all of the cases the motivation was sexual; however, DNA was infrequently found.
- 83.9% of the time, the offender was familiar with the contact site.
- In almost half of the cases the actual assault took place in the offender's home.
- There were multiple causes of death within this pathway which included Asphyxiation (n = 3); Blunt Force Trauma (n = 6); Drowning (n = 2); Gunshot Wounds (n = 2); Smothering (n = 2); Stab Wounds (n = 5); Strangulation (n = 10); and Undetermined (n = 4).
- In 41.9% of the cases, bindings were used.
- The majority of disposal sites were outdoor public areas and the offenders drove a vehicle to the disposal site.

Investigative Suggestions

- Approximately one third of the victims were prostitutes and the neighborhood investigation should focus on the areas the victims worked to ascertain possible suspects who frequented the area.
- Since most of the disposal sites were outdoor scenes, the neighborhood investigation should focus on the disposal areas to determine who would frequent the area.
- Investigative strategy should focus on media releases that provide information concerning the murders.

Pathway #2: Transported from the Murder Site and Dumped

A total of 8 offenders utilized this pathway murdering 38 victims.

These cases occurred when victims' bodies were transported from murder sites and the bodies were dumped, either alongside a road, or in another public area, with no attempt to conceal the victims. Offenders who dump victims' bodies do so because they are confident there is no recognizable connection between themselves and the victims. Again, the movement of the victims' bodies by offenders increases the chances that an offender may be seen or identified in the vicinity of the murder site and/or disposal site. This movement is extremely risky for an offender, yet these offenders are compelled to move the victims to place time and distance between themselves and the victims.

Frequent Occurrences within Pathway #2

Offenders

- Half were Black.
- Five of the eight offenders were between the ages of 21-26.
- Over half were not married.
- Half were employed full-time.
- Half of the offenders had education beyond high school.
- The majority did not serve in the military.
- None had a psychiatric diagnosis prior to the murders.
- The majority had a criminal history.
- The majority killed more than three victims.

Victims

- Most victims were White and between 14 and 29 years of age.
- Over one-third of the cases were male victims.
- Twelve of the 38 victims were prostitutes.

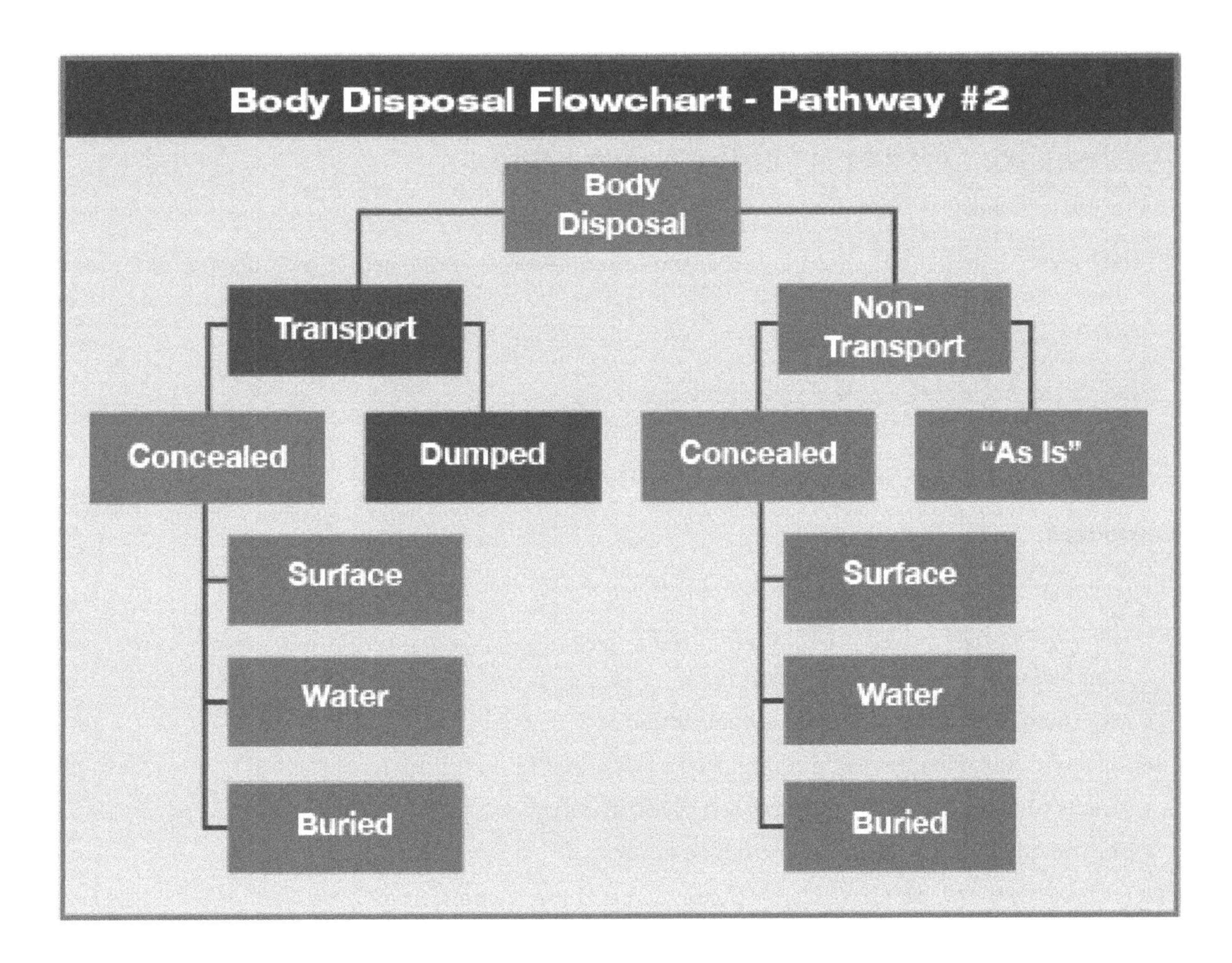

Crime Scene

- In the cases where the approach is known, all of the offenders utilized a ruse approach.
- The primary motivation was overwhelmingly sexual and DNA was found in approximately half of the cases.
- In only five cases, bindings were used.
- In over half of the cases, the cause of death was strangulation.
- In more than half of the cases, the victim was found fully or partially dressed.
- In all but three cases, the disposal sites were outdoor public areas.

Investigative Suggestions

- In the dumped scenario, the offender was not concerned that the victim may be discovered. This indicated the nature of the relationship was casual, and the offender may not have been known to the victim. Based on these circumstances, the investigation should focus on the last known activities of the victim to help determine how the offender identified the victim.

- The focus in these cases is determining how the offender is familiar with the dumpsite and their prior activity at the location prior to the body disposal.

Pathway #3: Left "As Is" at the Murder Site

A total of 24 offenders utilized this pathway murdering 97 victims.

Offenders who utilized this body disposal scenario committed the murder and the body disposal at the same site. They made no attempt to hide or conceal the victims' bodies and did not take any additional risks by moving them.

This was the most common body disposal scenario.

Frequent Occurrences within Pathway #3

Offenders

- Over half of the offenders were Black and between the ages of 15 and 37.
- The majority were not married at the time of the murder.
- Over half were employed at least part-time.
- More than half had at least a high school education.
- Eight of the 24 offenders had prior military service.
- Twenty nine percent of the offenders had psychiatric diagnosis prior to the homicide.
- The overwhelming majority had a criminal history.
- Over 40.0% of the offenders killed between three and four victims.

Victims

- Over half of victim's were White.
- Victims were six times more likely to be over 45 years of age than in any other pathway; over half were between the ages of 14 and 29.
- The majority of victims were female.
- Thirty-one of the 97 victims were prostitutes.

Crime Scene

- Of the cases known, offenders primarily utilized the ruse/con approach to gain access to the victims.
- The primary motivation was sexual and DNA was found in less than half of the cases.
- Most victims were found fully or partially dressed, with only a few (n = 16) found completely nude.
- The relationship between the offenders and the victims was primarily stranger or targeted stranger.
- Almost half of the victims were left in an outdoor/public area, and over one third of the victims were left in their residences.

Investigative Suggestions

- The focus in cases such as these is to identify the manner in which the offender identifies and targets the victims.
- Given the offender left the victim in the same location of the murder, a complete and thorough canvass of the area is needed to identify possible witnesses.
- As with every pathway, a complete victimology is central to a robust investigation in this pathway.

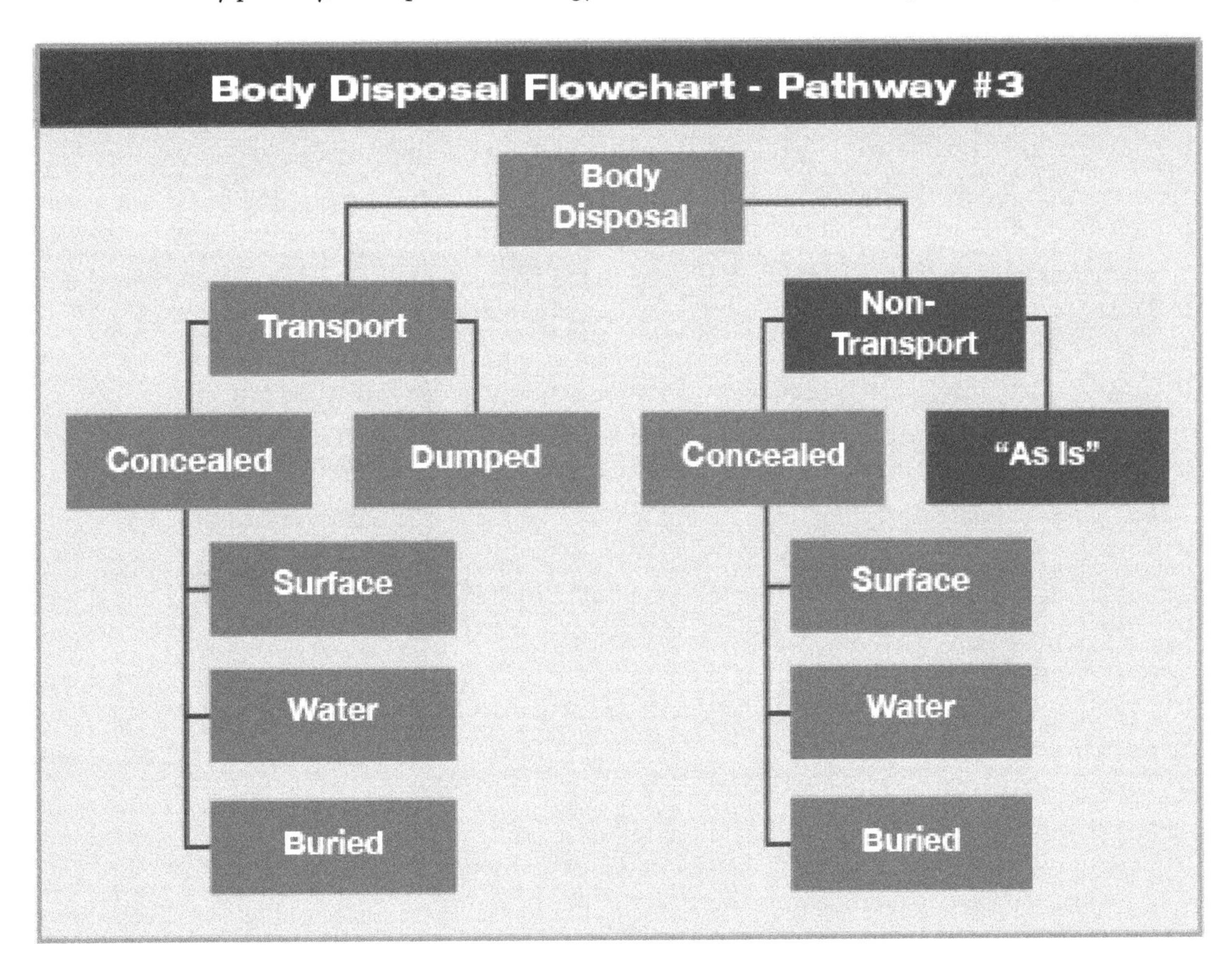

Pathway #4: Left at the Murder Site and Concealed

A total of zero offenders utilized this pathway.

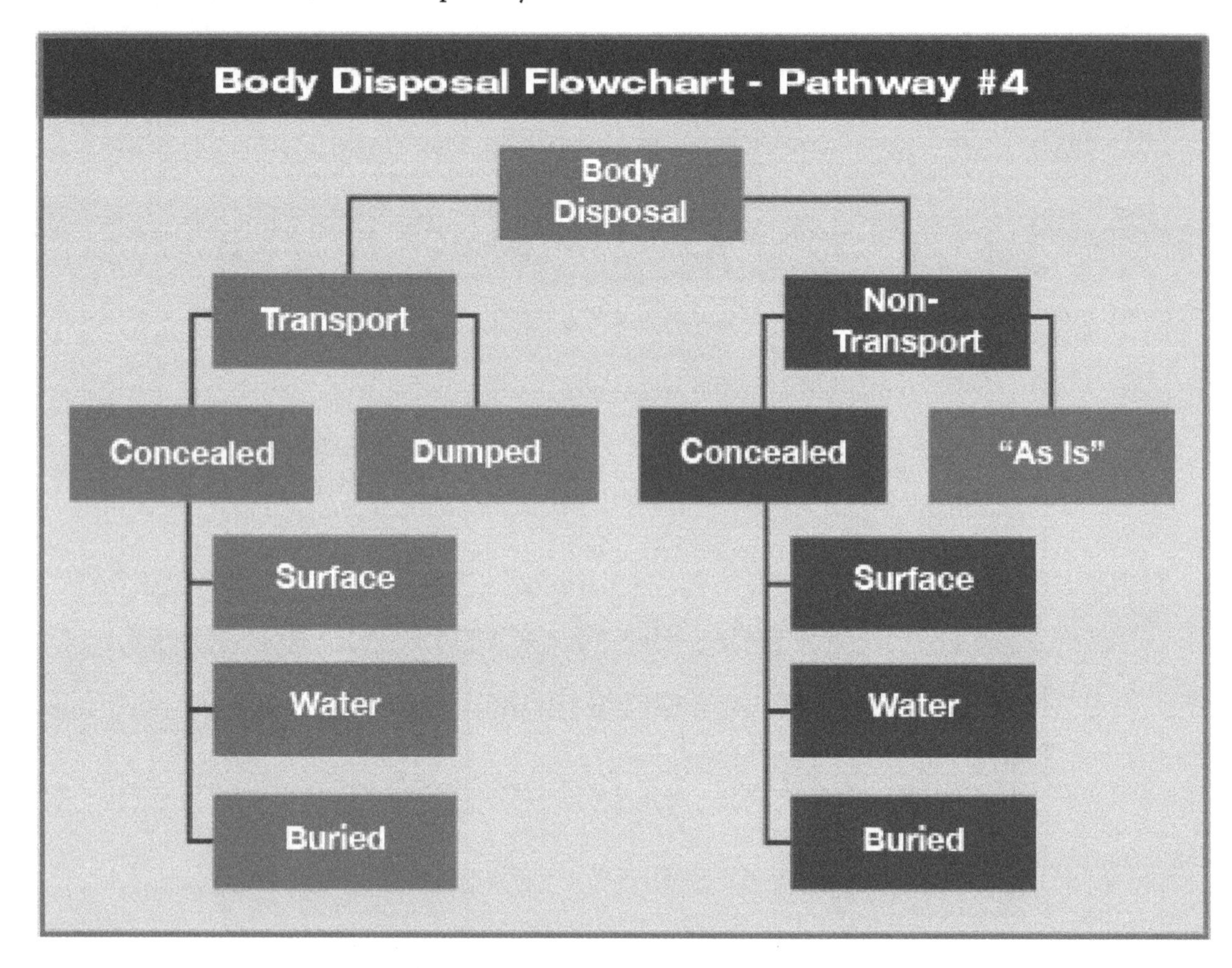

VI.

Offenders Who Changed Pathways

VI. Offenders Who Changed Pathways

In an effort to avoid or delay detection by law enforcement, the offender may change certain activities from one murder to another. Within our sample, 48 offenders utilized different pathways in their murder series, accounting for 293 victims. Some serial killers do not want law enforcement to know they are actively killing victims because this increases their risk of being detected. If there is no active investigation, they are free to continue their activities uninhibited. Also, widespread attention by the media highlighting that a serial killer is operating will make it more difficult for the offender to find more victims. Additionally, an offender may also change pathways for other reasons to include:

- The first disposal technique was too risky.
- Exigent circumstances (offender was interrupted).
- Available resources at the time of the murder.
- Publicity in the media identifying a particular disposal location or scenario.
- The presence of law enforcement near the disposal area.
- For personal reasons or some intrinsic need of the offender.

Among offenders who did change pathways, over three-quarters of offenders used two different pathways. Despite the change in disposal pathways, there were very minimal differences among victim characteristics and crime scene behaviors across the series.

The break out of pathways exhibited by these offenders is as follows:

Pathway #1: Transported from the Murder Site and Concealed

Total of 62 victims in this pathway.

- Surface: Total of 35 victims
- Water: Total of 20 victims
- Buried: Total of 7 victims

Pathway #2: Transported from the Murder Site and Dumped

Total of 81 victims in this pathway.

Pathway #3: Left "As Is" at the Murder Site

Total of 111 victims in this pathway.

Pathway #4: Left at the Murder Site and Concealed

Total of 31 victims in this pathway.

- Surface: Total of 24 victims
- Water: Total of 2 victims
- Buried: Total of 5 victims

Additionally, 8 victims' bodies were not recovered.

Unlike offenders who choose to maintain the same pathway throughout their series, Pathway #4: Left at the Murder Site and Concealed was only utilized by offenders who changed pathways.

Offenders conceal bodies for two main reasons:

- To delay or prevent discovery
- In order to place time and distance between themselves and the victims

Characteristics of offenders who changed pathways:

- 54.2% were White
- 58.3% of were under the age of 37
- 54.2% had at least a high school education
- 64.6% were not married
- 54.2% were employed at least part-time
- 89.6% had been arrested prior to the murder
- 66.7% did not have a military history
- 52.1% did not have a psychiatric diagnosis prior to their first murder
- 41.7% killed 3 to 4 victims

Investigative Suggestions

When investigating a series in which the offender has used more than one body disposal technique, it is crucial to examine other similarities that may exist. These can include how the offender gained access to the victim; the activities the offender participated in with the victim; the method of killing; and common characteristics of the victims.

When circumstances vary from case to case it can be very difficult to establish or determine a pattern. Due to these factors, subject matter experts should be contacted to assist. The FBI's Behavioral Analysis Unit can provide case linkage analysis in these difficult cases.

VII.

Serial Sexual Murders

Sexually motivated murder has been the subject of numerous studies by academics, mental health professionals, researchers and law enforcement professionals. Historically, some of these studies have attempted to delineate specific types of sexual murder and have used terms such as lust murder, sexual homicide, lust killings, and sadistic killings. The sexual acts committed by these offenders against their victims can vary greatly. These include types of sex that are considered conventional, such as vaginal, anal, and oral sex. There are also a number of unconventional sexual acts including fetish behaviors and paraphilias. These include fetishism, postmortem mutilation, foreign object penetration, sexual sadism, necrophilia, cannibalism, and vampirism.

For the purposes of this study, sexual murder is defined as a murder where the motivation is sexual in nature. The definition was deliberately kept broad because of the unusual nature of sexually motivated murder and the involvement of a wide variety of sexual behaviors. The sex could be overt, unusual or very subtle. The means to determine a sexual motivation included the sexual acts, sadistic acts, and any other sexual practices that occurred. These included physical evidence of sexual contact including DNA, physical trauma to the sex organs, the victim's state of dress, the positioning of the victim by the offender, the nature of the other injuries suffered by the victim, and evidence of the offender's use of bindings. These variables were collectively used to determine a sexual motivation.

Victims

In this study, 329 of the 480 victims were killed by an offender who was sexually motivated. Female victims comprised 85.4% of these victims, male victims were 14.6% of this category.

The age range of the victims:

- 8 to 13 years (3.3%)
- 14 to 29 years (47.4%)
- 30 to 45 years (35.0%)
- Over 45 years (9.4%)

For sixteen of the victims, their age could not be determined.

The majority of the victims (88.2%) were under the age of 45 years.

The racial breakdown of the victims:

- White (52.0%)
- Black (38.9%)
- Hispanic (6.1%)
- Other (2.4%)

For two of the victims, their race could not be determined.

Offenders (n=64)

The racial make-up of offenders:

- White (48.4%)
- Black (42.2%)
- Hispanic (7.8%)
- Other (1.6%)

The offenders were between 15 and 45 years old.

Only 25% of offenders were married and 65.6% were employed either full time or part-time. Forty-five percent of offenders were either renting or owned their own home. The majority of offenders (64.1%) had a high school diploma or higher educational level; with 39.1% having some college education.

At the time of the first murder, over half (56.5%) of the serial sexual offenders had a prior arrest record as compared to other serial offenders (21.7%). Twenty five percent of serial sexual offenders had prior military service as compared to other serial offenders (7.6%).

Sixteen serial sexual offenders were formally diagnosed by a mental health professional with a psychiatric disorder.

Offender/Victim Relationships

The relationship between the victim and the offender:

- Customer/client (55.6%)
- Stranger or targeted stranger (30.4%)
- Acquaintance (10.3%)

There were three cases involving a relative or family member. In nine cases, the relationship between the victim and offender could not be determined.

Race distribution of serial sexual offenders and their victims

Victim Race (n=329)	Offender Race		
	White	Black	Other**
White (n=171)	34.0%	12.8%	5.2%
Black (n=128)	12.8%	24.9%	1.2%
Other* (n=28)	4.9%	1.8%	1.8%
Unknown (n=2)	0.6%	-	-

**Other victim races include Hispanic, Asian and Native American.*
***Other offender races include Hispanic and Asian.*

Offense Characteristics

Of the 64 serial sexual offenders, 70.4% killed three or more victims with 39.1 % of them killing five or more victims.

The offenders approach to gain access to victims:

- Ruse/con (77.8%)
- Surprise (10.0%)
- Blitz (4.0%)
- Unknown (7.9%)

Location where offenders gained access to victims:

- Known vice areas (43.2%)
- Outdoor public areas (23.7%)
- Victims' residences (16.1%)
- Other (8.8%)
- Unknown (8.2%)

Other locations include interior public business/area, offender's residence, and other living quarters.

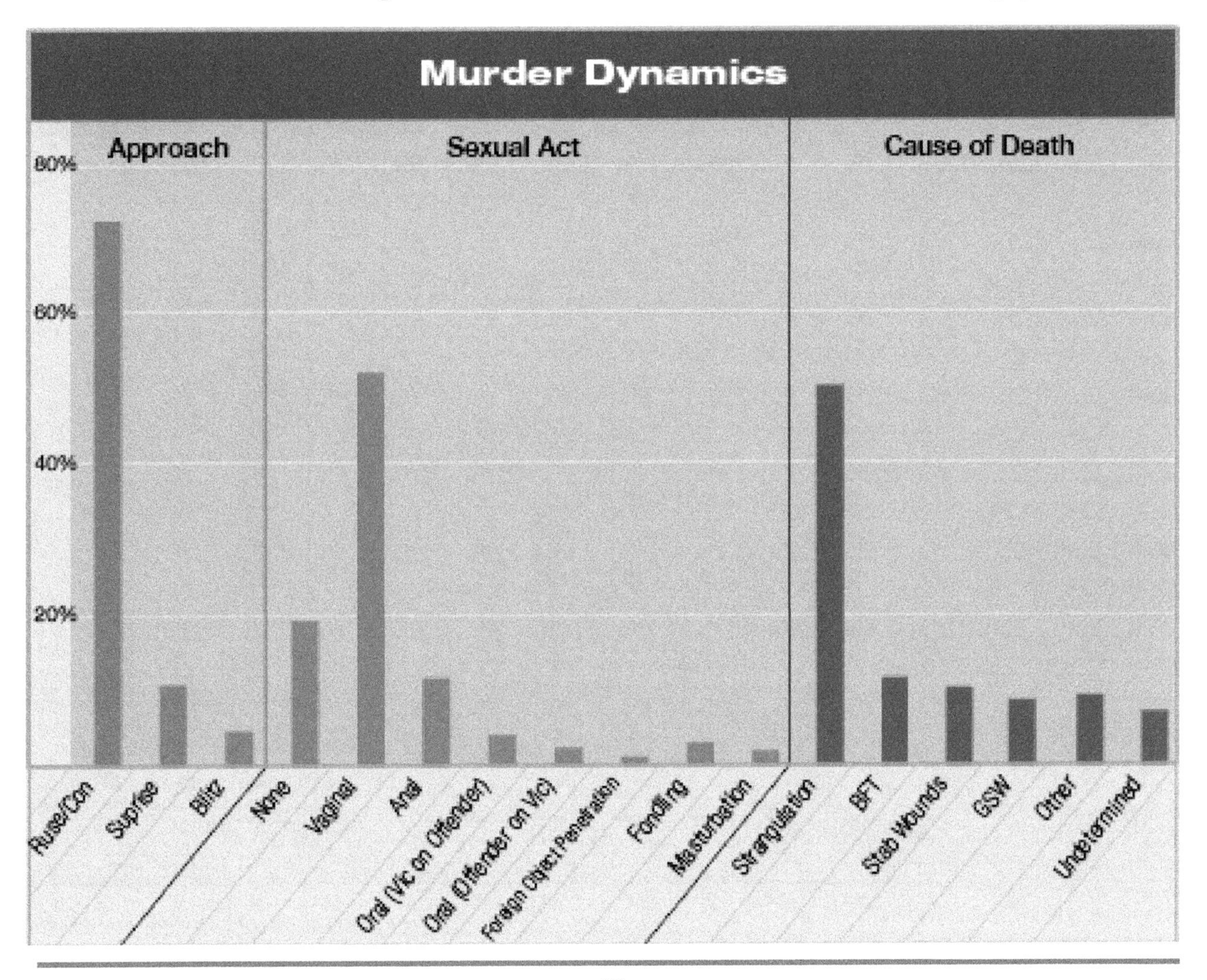

The locations where the sexual assaults took place:

- Outdoor public areas (23.4%)
- Offenders' residences (21.6%)
- Victims' residences (15.5%)
- Offenders' vehicles (17.6%)
- Unknown (15.2%)
- Other (6.7%)

Other locations include interior public business/area and other living quarters.

In 63.2% of the cases, the offender drove to the murder site.

The murder locations:

- Outdoor public areas (27.7%)
- Offenders' residences (21.3%)
- Victims' residences (15.8%)
- Offenders' vehicles (14.0%)
- Unknown (16.4%)
- Other (4.8%)

Other locations include interior public business/area and other living quarters.

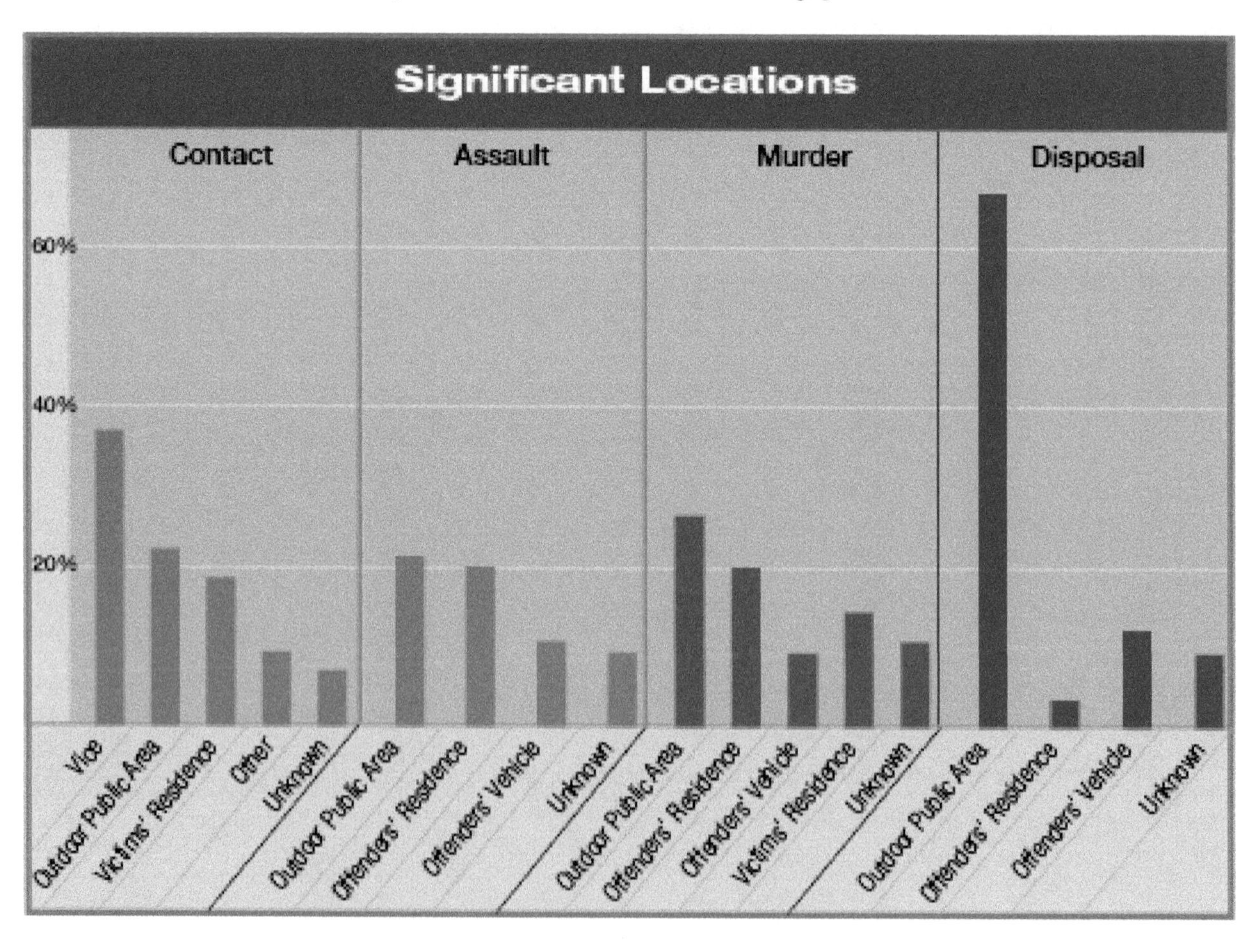

The specific disposal sites:

- Outdoor public areas (72.6%)
- Victims' residences (14.6%)
- Offenders' residences (2.4%)
- Other (7.0%)
- Unknown (3.3%)

Other locations include interior public business/area and other living quarters.

Additionally, six victims were not recovered.

The causes of death:

- Strangulation (51.6%)
- Blunt force trauma (13.7%)
- Stab wounds (10.6%)
- Gunshot wounds (7.6%)
- Undetermined (9.1%)
- Other (0.6%)
- Unknown (4.9%)

The Undetermined category was ruled by a medical examiner.

In 75.1% of the cases, the victims were found nude or partially nude.

There was evidence of sexual contact in 49.5% of cases, and DNA was recovered in 29.2% of the cases and was found in the victim, on the victim, or at the crime scene. There was evidence of postmortem sexual activity in 11.2% of the cases.

The number of cases in which DNA was recovered (29.2%) was much higher as compared to other serial offenders whose DNA was only recovered in 2.7% of the cases. This highlights the need for law enforcement to utilize proper recovery techniques when processing sexually motivated murders.

Bindings were utilized in 31.3% of the cases. Offenders took objects in 53.8% of the cases and clothing was the most commonly taken item.

There were eight instances of unusual sexual acts such as foreign object penetration.

Time Frames

The time frame was calculated between when the murders occurred and when the victims' bodies were recovered.

- Victims found less than one day after murder (31.3%)
- Victims found between one and fifteen days (27.7%)
- Victims found after fifteen days (10.2%)
- In 30.8% of the cases, the time frame could not be determined

There is a distinct contrast in time frames when examining serial sexual murderers and the other types of offenders in this sample. Among serial sexual murders, bodies recovered within 15 days occurred in 59.0% of cases versus 23.3% of other cases. Additionally, among sexual serial murder cases, victims recovered in less than one day occurred in 31.3% of cases versus 12.7% of other cases.

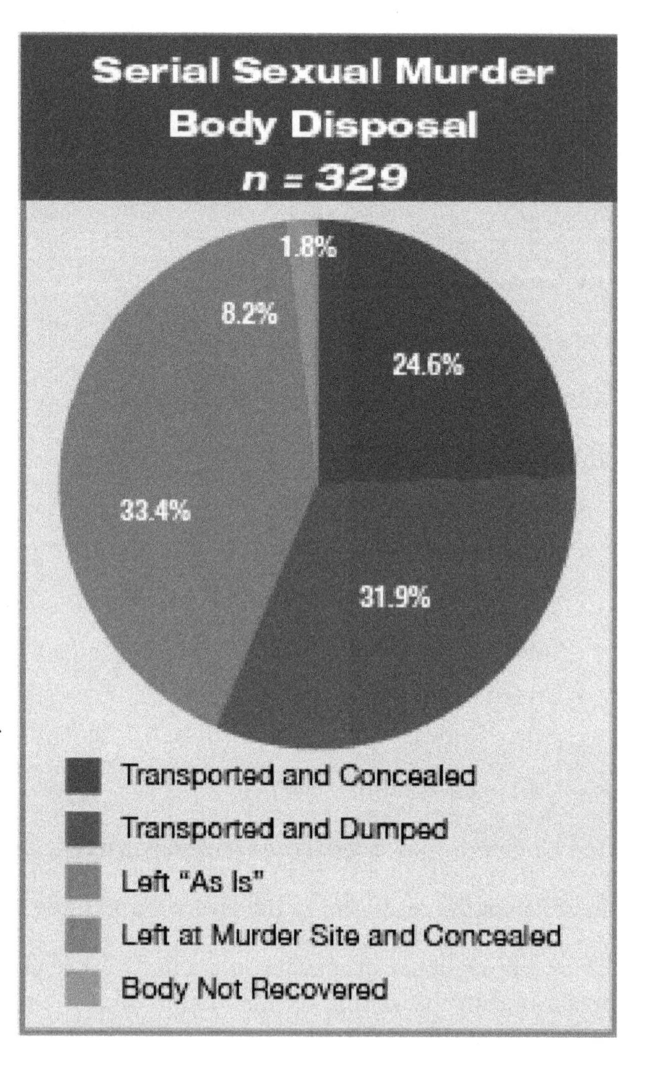

Body Disposal (n=329)

Transported and Concealed (24.6%)

- Surface (12.2%)
- Water (8.8%)
- Burial (3.6%)

Transported and Dumped (31.9%)

Left "As Is" at the Murder Site (33.4%)

Left at the Murder Site and Concealed (8.2%)

Body Not Recovered (1.8%)

In sexually motivated murders, there were more instances of offenders transporting their victims than other types of murders.

Refer to Chapter III for comprehensive investigative guidelines.

VIII.

Serial Prostitute Murders

Serial prostitute victims are a subset of serial sexual murder, discussed in the previous chapter. Prostitutes are considered high risk victims because of the nature of their work in which they engage in sex acts with total strangers for money. They are also visible and easily identifiable for a would-be offender as they are frequently located in areas known for prostitution activities. A large portion of them are drug and/or alcohol dependant and their judgment could be impaired. Also, their judgement regarding who they will engage in sex with can be clouded by their need to obtain substances to fuel their drug/alcohol dependency. Some prostitutes also have a very transitory life style and are not accountable to anyone for large blocks of time. It can be extremely difficult to track the activities of someone engaged in this lifestyle. All of these factors increase the risk prostitutes may become the target of a serial killer.

Additionally, the murder of a prostitute can be very challenging for law enforcement investigators to solve. The covert nature of the sexual activities, coupled with the number of interactions with strangers makes identification of any customers who may be critical witnesses extremely difficult.

Victims (n = 154)

In this study, 154 of the 480 victims were engaged in prostitution activities, and the majority of victims were female (84.4%).

The age range of victims:

- 14 to 29 years (37.0%)
- 30 to 45 years (48.1%)
- Over 45 years (7.1%)
- Unknown (7.8%)

The racial breakdown of the victims:

- White (27.9%)
- Black (64.3%)
- Hispanic (5.8%)
- Other (1.3%)
- Unknown (0.6%)

Offenders (n = 27)

The racial make-up of offenders:

- Black (55.6%)
- White (33.3%)
- Hispanic (7.4%)
- Other (3.7%)

The offenders were between 21 and 43 years old. Descriptors are based upon the first murder in the series.

At the time of the first murder, 25.9% of offenders were married and 40.7% lived as dependents of either family members or paramours, with 14.8% of offenders being homeless.

Over half of the offenders (51.8%) had a high school diploma or higher educational level, with 40.7% having some college education. Less than a quarter (22.2%) had prior military service and 70.4% were employed either part or full time at the time of the first homicide.

The majority of offenders had a prior arrest record (92.6%) and only 11.1% were formally diagnosed by a mental health professional with a psychiatric disorder.

Offender/Victim Relationships

The relationship between all of the offenders and the victims were customer/client (100.0%).

Offense Characteristics

Of the 27 offenders, 66.6% of them killed three or more victims, with 37.0% of them killing five or more victims.

Race distribution of serial prostitute offenders and their victims

Victim Race (n=154)	Offender Race		
	White	Black	Other**
White (n=43)	17.5%	7.1%	3.2%
Black (n=99)	22.1%	39.6%	2.6%
Other* (n=11)	5.2%	-	1.9%
Unknown (n=1)	0.6%	-	-

**Other victim races include Hispanic and Asian.*
***Other offender races include Hispanic and Asian.*

The majority of offenders (98.7%) utilized a ruse/con approach to gain access to the victims and in three-quarters (74.7%) of the cases, offenders made initial contact in known vice areas. All murders were sexually motivated.

The primary location where the initial assaults took place:

- Offenders' residences (34.4%)
- Outdoor public areas (23.4%)
- Offenders' vehicles (18.2%)

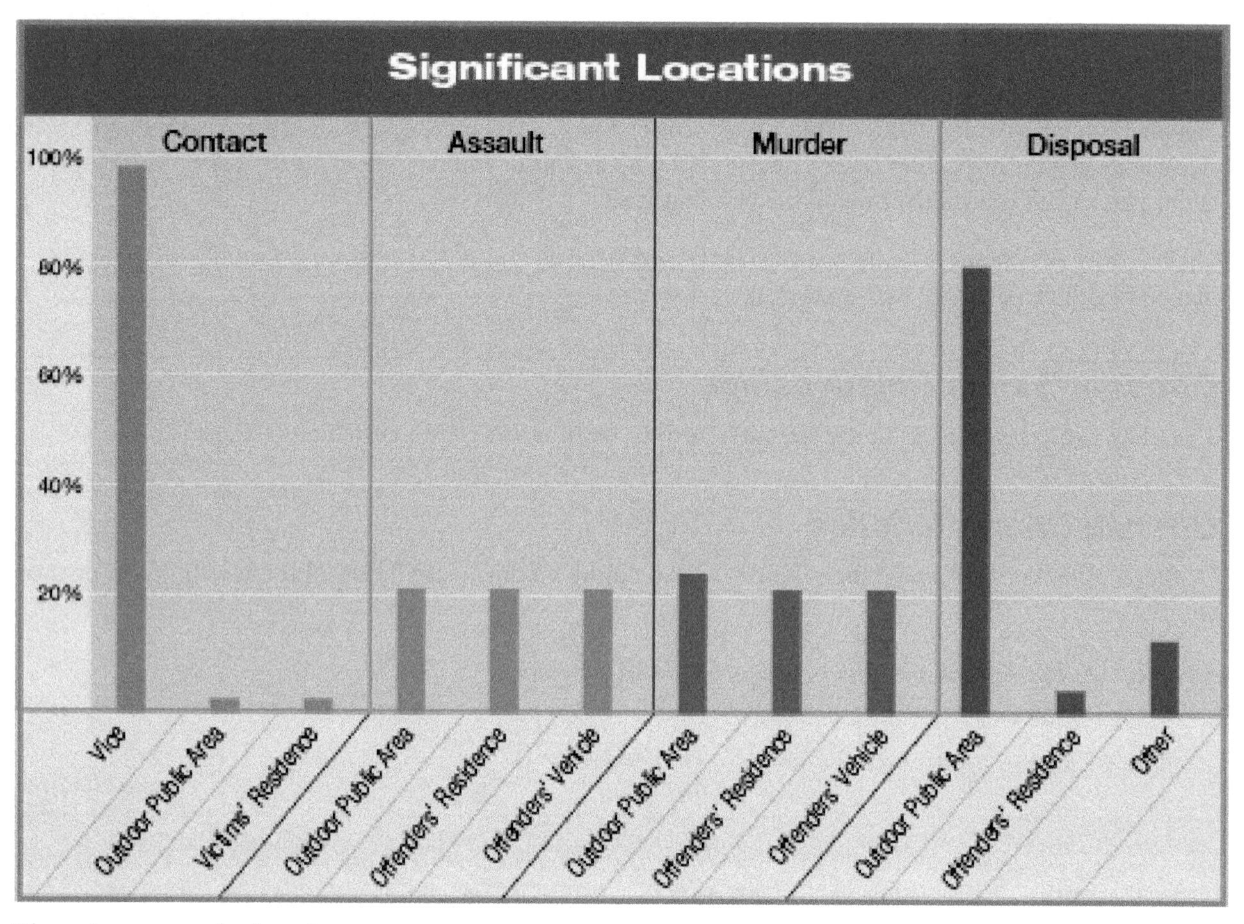

The primary murder locations:

- Offenders' residences (34.4%)
- Outdoor public areas (26.0%)
- Offenders' vehicles (17.5%)

Over 80% of all victims were killed and assaulted in the same location. In 65.6% of the cases, the offender drove to the murder site.

The specific disposal sites:

- Outdoor public areas (82.5%)
- Offenders' residences (5.2%)
- Other (8.4%)

Additionally, 2.6% of victims' bodies were not recovered.

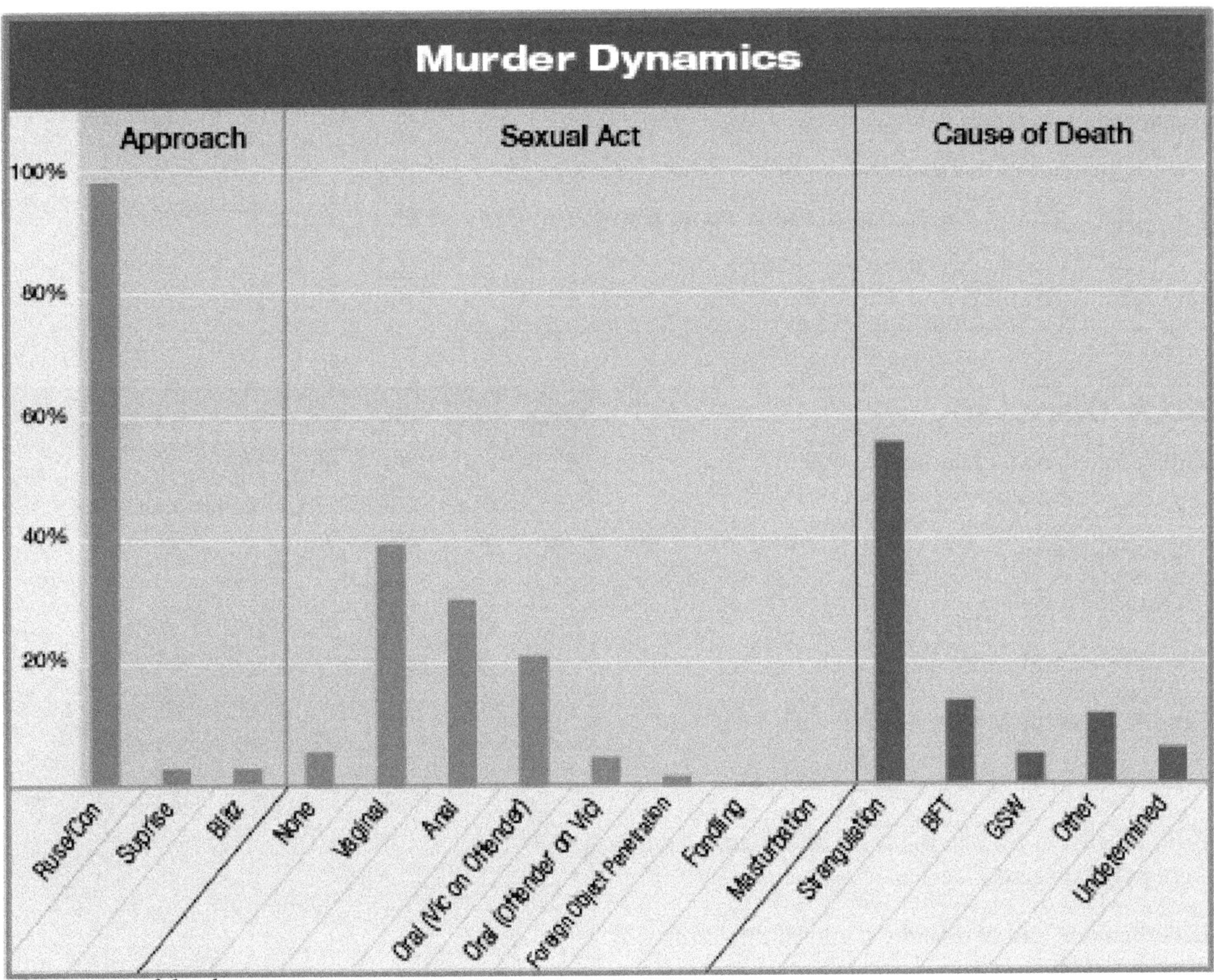

The causes of death:

- Strangulation (63.0%)
- Blunt force trauma (17.5%)
- Undetermined (10.4%)
- Other (3.9%)

In 5.2% of the cases, the victims' bodies were not recovered.

The Undetermined category was ruled by a medical examiner.

In 75.3% of the cases, the victims were found nude or partially nude.

There was evidence of sexual contact in 61.7% of cases and DNA found either in the victim, on the victim or at the crime scene in 28.6% of the cases. In addition, there was evidence of post-mortem mutilation on thirteen victims.

Time Frames

The time frame was calculated between when the murders occurred and when the victims' bodies were recovered.

- Victims found less than one day after murder (26.6%)
- Victims found between one and fifteen days (29.0%)
- Victims found after fifteen days (3.6%)

In 40.3% of the cases, the time frame could not be determined.

Body Disposal

Transported and Concealed (26.0%)

- Surface (13.6%)
- Water (10.4%)
- Burial (1.9%)

Transported and Dumped (37.0%)

Left "As Is" at the Murder Site (29.9%)

Left at the Murder Site and Concealed (4.5%)

Additionally, in 2.6% of the cases, the victims' bodies were not recovered.

Less than one half of offenders utilized different body disposal scenarios.

**Refer to Chapter III for comprehensive investigative guidelines.*

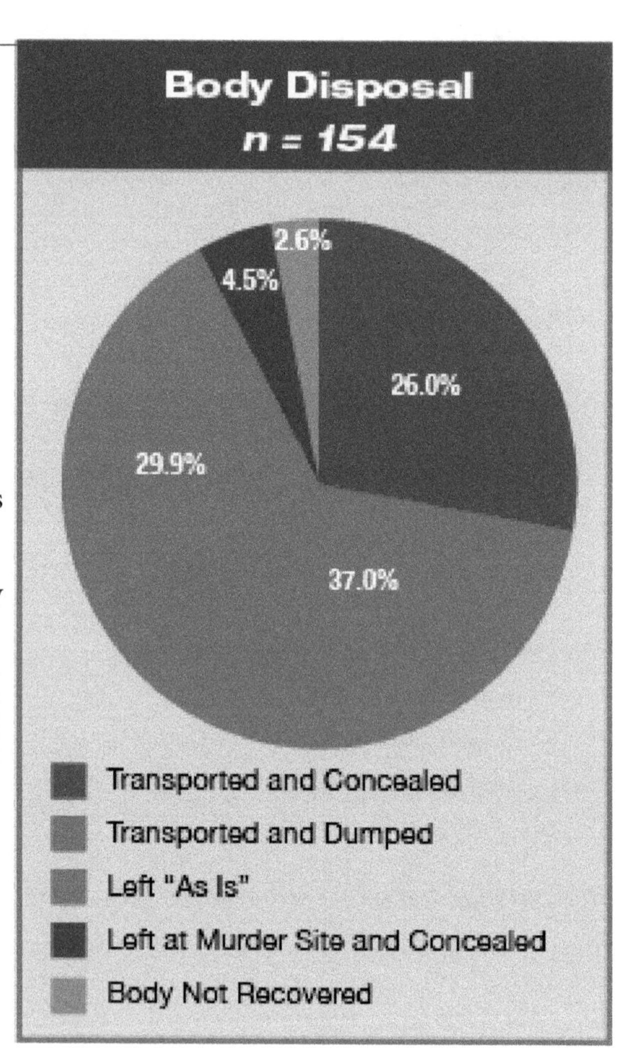

IX.

Serial Same Sex Murders

Within this study, seven offenders targeted only males; twenty-one offenders targeted both genders and sixty four offenders targeted only females. Offenders who only target male victims represent a small but unique subset of this study. They represent an unusual scenario within serial murder and pose distinctive investigative challenges. This chapter will highlight the seven offenders who killed a total of 68 male victims. As stated previously, the primary motive was determined after a complete review of the case materials. The primary motivation was determined to be sexual (85.3%). The motivations for the murders were:

- Sexual (85.3%)
- Profit (5.9%)
- Mental Illness (4.4%)
- Anger (1.5%)
- Unknown (3.0%)

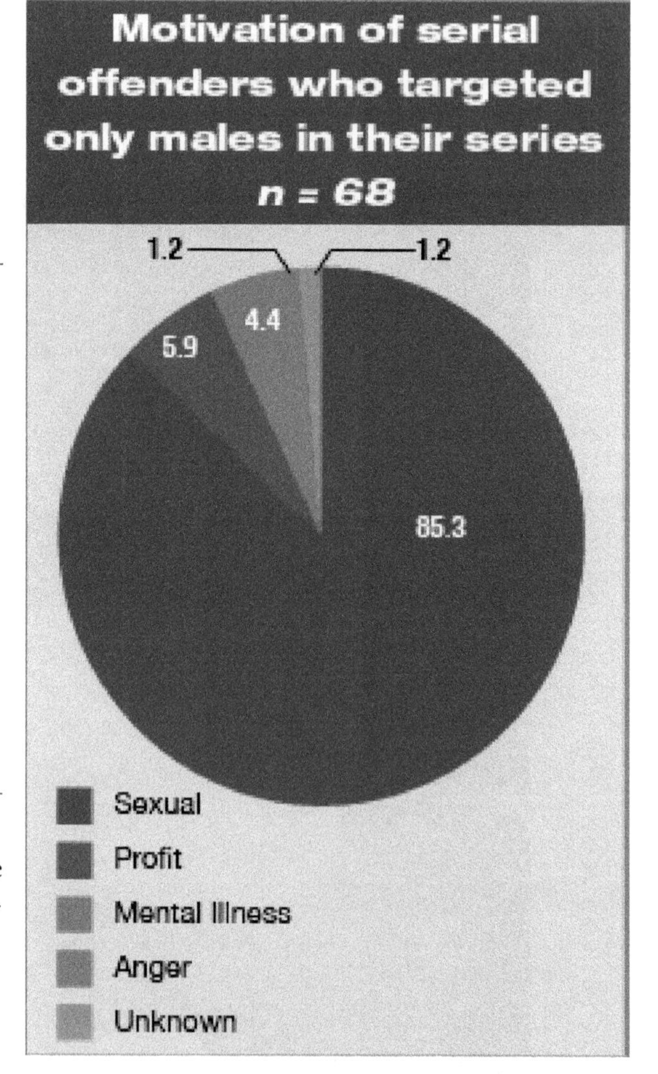

Victims (n = 68)

The age range of victims:

- 8 to 13 years (2.9%)
- 14 to 29 years of age (63.2%)
- 30 to 45 years of age (26.5%)
- Over 45 years of age (7.4%)

The racial breakdown of the victims:

- Black (50.0%)
- White (39.7%)
- Other (10.2)

Offenders (n = 7)

The small number of offenders precludes using the offender data for anything other than general information. The racial make-up for offenders:

- White (57.1%)
- Black (42.9%)

Offenders were between 18 and 35 years old at the time of their first murder. Only one offender was married, and most were living as dependents of either family members or paramours. Most offenders had high school or further formal education; however, less than half were unemployed. Additionally, two offenders had prior military service.

Most had a previous arrest; with the primary offenses being sex offenses, assault, and DUI/DWI. Less than one-half of the offenders were previously diagnosed with a psychiatric disorder prior to the start of their murders.

Offender/Victim Relationships

The relationship between the victim and the offender:

- Customer/client (45.6%)
- Stranger or targeted stranger (26.5%)
- Acquaintance (19.1%)

Offense Characteristics

In 85.5% of the cases, offenders killed three or more victims, with 71.5% of offenders killing five or more victims.

Race distribution of serial same sex offenders and their victims

Victim Race (n=68)	Offender Race	
	White	Black
White (n=27)	26.5%	39.7%
Black (n=34)	13.2%	10.3%
Other* (n=7)	8.8%	1.5%

**Other victim races include Hispanic and Asian.*

The majority of offenders utilized a ruse/con approach (86.8%) to gain access to the victims, with only 2.9% utilizing a blitz approach, and the remainder being unknown.

The locations where offenders gained access to victims:

- Outdoor public areas (52.9%)
- Interior public locations (23.5%)
- Unknown (16.2%)
- Other (7.4%)

The locations where the assaults and murders took place:

- Offenders' residences (48.5%)
- Offenders' vehicles (14.7%)
- Victims' residences (7.4%)
- Other (13.2%)
- Unknown (16.2%)

Other assault areas include interior public business/area, outdoor public areas, and other living quarters.

The specific disposal sites:

- Outdoor public areas (61.8%)
- Offenders' residences (14.7%)
- Other living quarters (11.8%)
- Victims' residences (7.4%)
- Interior public area (2.9%)
- Unknown (1.5%)

The causes of death:

- Strangulation (67.6%)
- Blunt force trauma (11.8%)
- Gunshot wounds (4.4%)
- Stab wounds (2.9%)
- Other (5.9%)
- Undetermined (7.4%)

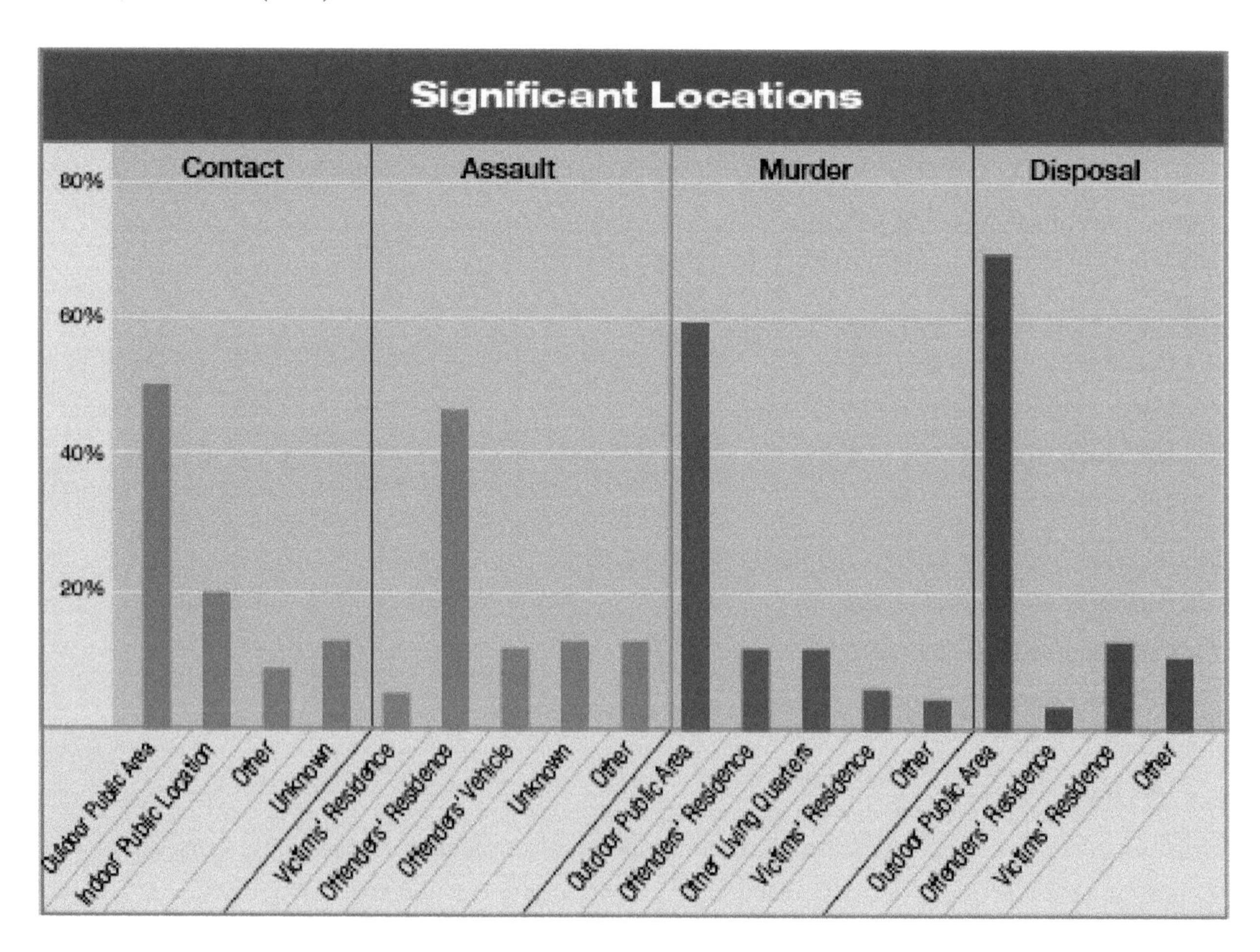

Over half of the victims (51.5%) were found nude or partially nude, and 17.6% of the victims were re-dressed by the offender.

The evidence of sexual contact varied, with anal sex occurring in 39.7% of the cases, the offender performing oral sex on the victim (19.1%), fondling (19.1%), the victim performing oral sex on the offender (17.6%), and masturbation (16.2%). No DNA was found in 80.9% of the cases. Offenders' used bindings in 36.8% of the cases. Additionally, there was evidence of post mortem sex in 20.6%, and post-mortem mutilation in 26.5% of the cases.

Offenders took items in less than half of the cases (47.0%), with clothing (36.8%) being the most commonly taken item.

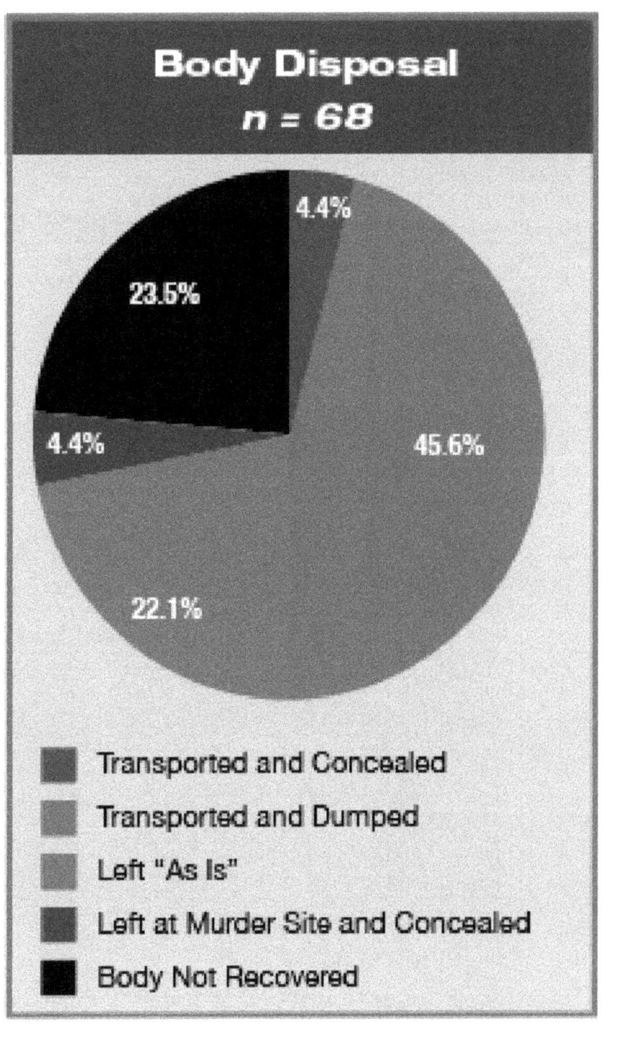

Time Frames

A comparison was conducted regarding when the murders occurred and when the victims' bodies were recovered:

- Victims found less than one day after murders (13.2%)
- Victims found between one and fifteen days (47.1%)
- Victims found after fifteen days (17.6%)

In 22.1% of the cases, the time frame could not be determined.

Body Disposal

- Transported and Concealed (4.4%)
- Left "As Is" at the Murder Site (22.1%)
- Left at the Murder Site and Concealed (4.4%)

Additionally, in 23.5% of the cases, victims' bodies were not recovered.

It is recommended that investigators seek the assistance of the FBI's NCAVC to provide guidance in these type of investigations.

X.

Multiple Motivations

There are many motivations for serial murder and each presents unique challenges for law enforcement investigating these complex cases. When the killers' motivations change from case to case, this creates problematic issues linking multiple victims to the same offender. In this study, sixteen offenders were found to have killed 97 victims for different motivations during their murder series. Male victims account for 57.7% of the sample.

Please refer to pages 15 and 16 for the authors' discussion and definitions on motivations identified throughout the study.

Victims (n=97)

The age range of victims:

- 8 to13 years (5.2%)
- 14 to 29 years (51.5%)
- 30 to 45 years (18.6%)
- Over 45 years (24.7%)

Three quarters of victims (75.3%) were under the age of 45 years.

The racial breakdown of the victims:

- White (78.4%)
- Black (12.4%)
- Hispanic (5.2%)
- Other (4.1%)

Offenders (n=16)

The racial breakdown of offenders:

- White (56.3%)
- Black (31.3%)
- Hispanic (12.5%)

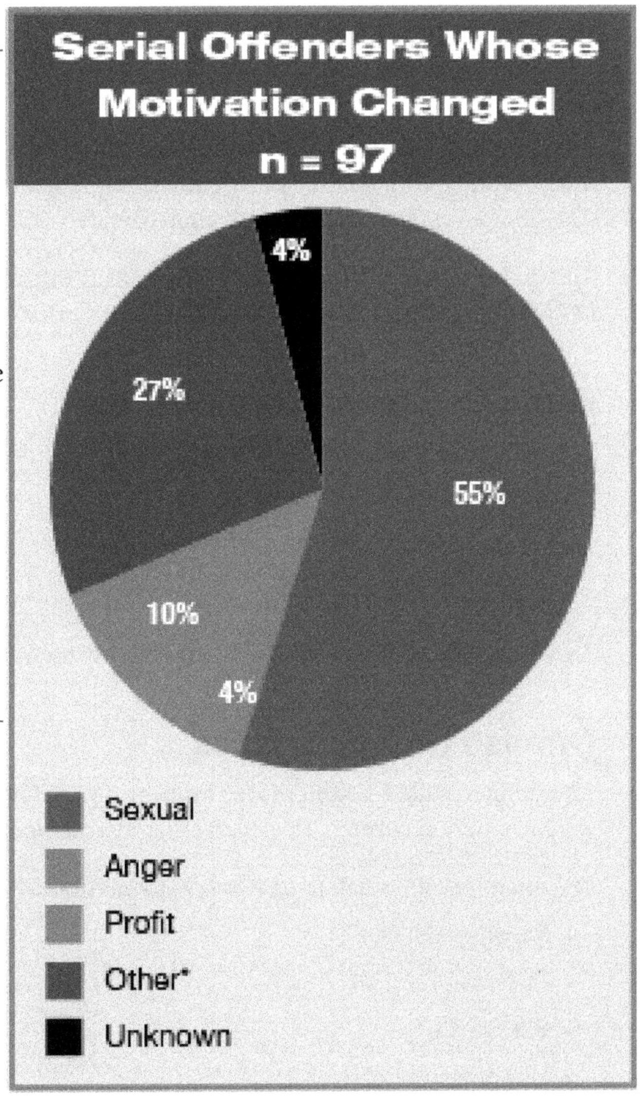

**Other category consists of cases involving witness elimination (17.5%); to gain access to the primary victims' significant other or family member for the*

Race distribution of offenders and their victims

Victim Race (n=97)	Offender Race		
	White	Black	Hispanic
White (n=76)	35.1%	29.9%	13.4%
Black (n=12)	9.3%	2.1%	1.0%
Other* (n=9)	8.2%	-	1.0%

**Other victim races include Hispanic, Asian and Native American.*

At the time of the first murder, offenders were between 16 and 36 years old. Three quarters of them were not married and over a quarter were living as dependents (31.3%). Over half (62.5%) had a high school diploma or higher level of education; with approximately 25% having some college education.

The majority had a prior arrest history (81.3%) and had no prior military service (81.3%). Six offenders (37.5%) had a diagnosed psychiatric disorder prior to their first murder.

Offender/Victim Relationships

The relationship between the victim and the offender:

- Stranger or targeted stranger (79.3%)
- Acquaintance (11.3%)
- Customer/client (8.2%)

There was one case involving a relative/family member.

Offense Characteristics

All offenders killed 3 or more victims, with 43.8% killing 5 or more victims. Of note, eighteen victims' bodies were not fully recovered. In eleven cases, partial body parts (skull/head, torso) were found.

The offenders approach to gain access to victims:

- Surprise (44.3%)
- Ruse/con (35.1%)
- Blitz (6.2%)
- Unknown (14.4%)

Location where the offenders gained access to victims:

- Victims' residences (48.5%)
- Outdoor Public Area (21.6%)
- Interior Public Business/Area (17.5%)
- Living Quarters/Other (5.2%)
- Unknown (5.2%)
- Offenders' residences (1.0%)
- Vice Area (1.0%)

Location where the assaults took place:

- Victims' residences (44.3%)
- Outdoor Public Area (18.6%)
- Offenders' residences (17.5%)
- Living Quarters/Other (9.3%)
- Unknown (5.2%)
- Interior Public Business/Area (4.1%)
- Offenders' Vehicle (1.0%)

The murder locations:

- Victims' residences (44.3%)
- Outdoor Public Area (19.6%)
- Offenders' residences (15.5%)
- Living Quarters/Other (6.2%)
- Unknown (6.2%)
- Interior Public Area (5.2%)
- Offenders' vehicle (3.1%)

Specific disposal sites:

- Victims' residences (42.3%)
- Outdoor Public Area (30.9%)
- Offenders' residences (10.3%)
- Living Quarters/Other (10.3%)
- Interior Public Area (4.1%)
- Unknown/Body Not Recovered (2.1%)

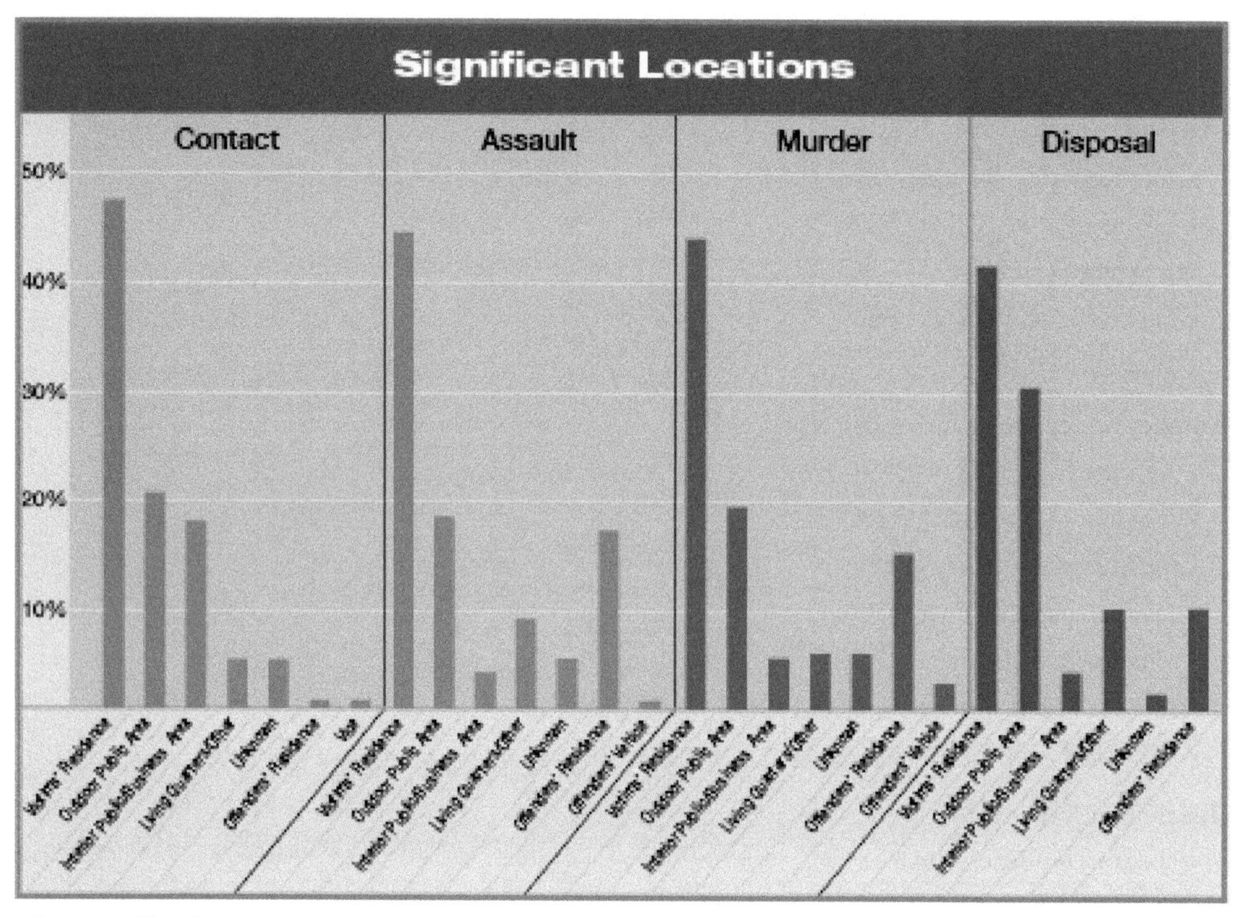

Causes of death:

- Strangulation (26.8%)
- Gunshot wounds (24.7%)
- Blunt force trauma (22.7%)
- Stab wounds (20.6%)
- Other (3.1%)
- Unknown (1.0%)
- Body not recovered (1.0%)

In 44.4% of the cases, the victims were found nude or partially nude. In 36.1% of the cases they were found fully dressed. Although eighteen victims' bodies were not recovered, a skull was actually recovered in nine cases.

Over half (51.5%) of the victims whose bodies were recovered showed no evidence of sexual contact and in 11.3%, DNA was recovered in the victim or elsewhere at the crime scene. Offenders took items in 55.7% of the cases, with the items ranging from personal effects (clothing, letters, money and jewelry) to victims' vehicles.

Bindings were utilized in 74.2% of the cases and evidence of post mortem sexual activity in 21.6% of the cases. Unusual trauma or torture occurred in 46.4% of the cases which included cannibalism, evisceration, burning, skinning, hanging, bite marks and mutilation of body cavities or genitalia.

Time Frames

The time frame was calculated between when the murders occurred and when the victims' bodies were recovered. In eleven cases, the time frame was unknown.

- Victims found less than one day after murder (38.1%)
- Victims found between one and fifteen days (36.1%)
- Victims found after fifteen days (14.0%)

Body Disposal

- Transported and Concealed (8.2%)
  - Surface (7.2%)
  - Burial (1.0%)
- Transported and Dumped (4.1%)
- Left "As Is" at the Murder Site (64.9%)
- Left at the Murder Site and Concealed (4.1%)
- Body Not Recovered (18.6%)
  - Partial recovery - skull/head, torso, or muscle tissue (11.3%)

It is important to remember in active serial murder investigations, motive may be difficult to determine. A serial murderer may have multiple motives and evolve throughout the murder series and utilizing investigative resources to discern the motive may derail the investigation from identifying the offender (Morton & Hilts, 2008). Serial homicide offenders who display different motivations for their murders can create problematic issues in linking cases. The NCAVC has uniquely qualified subject matter experts that can provide investigative and behavioral assistance in these types of cases.

Bibliography

Canter, D.V., Alison, L.J., Alison, E., & Wentink, N. (2004). The organized/disorganized typology of serial murder: Myth or model? *Psychology, Public Policy, and Law, 10*, 293-320.

Canter, D.V., & Wentink, N. (2004). An empirical test of Holmes and Holmes's serial murder typology. *Criminal Justice and Behavior, 31*, 489-515.

Centers for Disease Control and Prevention. (2011). Mental illness surveillance among adults in the United States. *Morbidity and Mortality Weekly Report, 60*, 129.

Chan, H.C., & Heide, K.M. (2009). Sexual homicide: A synthesis of the literature. *Trauma, Violence, and Abuse, 10*, 31-54.

Douglas, J.E., Burgess, A.W., Burgess, A.G., & Kessler, R.K. (1992). *Crime Classification Manual: A Standard System For Investigating and Classifying Violent Crimes.* New York: Lexington Books.

Douglas, J. & Olshaker, M. (1995). *Mind Hunter: Inside the FBI's Elite Serial Crime Unit.* New York: Scribner.

Federal Bureau of Investigation. (2010). Uniform Crime Report. Retrieved from http://www.fbi.gov/about-us/cjis/ucr/crime-in-the-u.s/2010/crime-in-the-u.s.2010.

Geberth. V. J. (1996). *Practical Homicide Investigation, 3rd Edition.* Boca Raton, FL: CRC.

Groth, A.N., Burgess, A.W., & Holmstrom, L.L. (1977). Rape: Power, anger, and sexuality. *The American Journal of Psychiatry, 134*, 1239-1243.

Hickey, E.W. (2002). *Serial Murderers and Their Victims (3rd ed.).* Belmont, CA: Wadsworth.

Holmes, R.M., & DeBurger, J. (1988). *Serial Murder: Studies in Crime, Law and Justice (Vol.2).* Newbury Park, CA: Sage.

Holmes, R.M., & Holmes, S.T. (2009). *Profiling Violent Crimes: An Investigative Tool (4th ed.).* Thousand Oaks, CA: Sage.

IBM Corp. Released 2011. *IBM SPSS Statistics for Windows, Version 20.0.* Armonk, NY: IBM Corp.

Keppel, R.D., & Walter, R. (1999). Profiling killers: A revised classification model for understanding sexual murder. *International Journal of Offender Therapy and Comparative Criminology, 43*, 417-437.

Meloy, J.R. (2000). The nature and dynamics of sexual homicide: An integrative review. *Aggression and Violent Behavior, 5*, 1-22.

Morton, R.J., & Hilts, M.A. (Eds.). (2008). *Serial Murder: Multi-Disciplinary Perspectives for Investigators.* Quantico, VA: Federal Bureau of Investigation.

Morton, R.J., & Lord, W.D. (2005). Criminal profiling. In J. Payne-James (Ed.), *Encyclopedia of Forensic and Legal Medicine* (pp. 51-55). Oxford: Elsevier Ltd.

Morton, R.J., & McNamara, J.J. (2005). Serial murder. In J. Payne-James (Ed.), *Encyclopedia of Forensic and Legal Medicine* (pp. 47-53). Oxford: Elsevier Ltd.

Ressler, R.K., Burgess, A.W., Douglas, J.E., Hartman, C.R., & D'Agostino, R.B. (1986). Sexual killers and their victims: Identifying patterns through crime scene analysis. *Journal of Interpersonal Violence, 1*, 288-308.

US Department of Health and Human Services, Office of the Surgeon General Center for Mental Health Services, National Institute of Mental Health. (1999). Mental health: *A report of the Surgeon General.* Retrieved from http://profiles.nlm.nih.gov/ps/retrieve/ ResourceMetadata/ NNBBHS

Biographical Information of Authors

Robert J. Morton, M.S.
Supervisory Special Agent

Supervisory Special Agent (SSA) Morton has a master's degree in Criminal Justice and been assigned to the Behavioral Analysis Unit, National Center for the Analysis of Violent Crime (NCAVC) since 1997. Prior to joining the FBI in 1988, SSA Morton was a trooper for the Virginia State Police and has previous experience working for the Federal Bureau of Prisons, and the New York State Department of Psychiatry and Mental Health. As a Supervisory Special Agent for the NCAVC, SSA Morton reviews investigations involving serial murder, sexual murder, and other types of homicides and sexual assaults involving adult victims that are submitted by law enforcement agencies for assistance. Since SSA Morton was assigned to the NCAVC, he has consulted in hundreds of these types of cases domestically, as well as a number of cases internationally. He has extensive experience analyzing homicide cases and other types of violent crimes, especially serial murder and sexual homicide. He routinely provides training to law enforcement and other criminal justice agencies on a variety of topics and has taught throughout the United States, Canada, and Europe. He is the Principal Investigator on several research projects including: characteristics of serial murderers, serial homicide interviews of incarcerated offenders, sexual murder, and sexual sadism.

Jennifer M. Tillman, M.A.
Crime Analyst

Crime Analyst (CA) Tillman has a master's degree in Forensic Psychology, and has been assigned to the Behavioral Analysis Unit, National Center for the Analysis of Violent Crime (NCAVC), since 2006. Prior to joining the NCAVC, CA Tillman was employed as a Domestic Violence Counselor for a non-profit agency that handled the Department of Correction contracts for the state of Connecticut. She conducted intake interviews and assessments, as well as provided group counseling, crisis intervention, and case management to court-mandated male offenders. CA Tillman also has experience as a Corrections Counselor where she provided individual counseling for criminal justice clients in a variety of settings including correctional institutions and alternative incarceration centers. As a Crime Analyst assigned to the NCAVC, CA Tillman works closely with Supervisory Special Agents on violent, criminal investigations that target adult victims. She provides detailed analytical packages consisting of maps, matrices, linkage charts, timelines and other database search results to investigators and prosecutors alike. CA Tillman is actively involved in on-going research projects regarding topics such as: characteristics of serial murderers, sexual murder, sexual sadism, and false allegation.

Stephanie J. Gaines, M.A.
Research Analyst

Stephanie J. Gaines has a master's degree in Forensic Psychology, and has been assigned to the FBI's Behavioral Analysis Unit, National Center for the Analysis of Violent Crime (NCAVC), since 2010. Mrs. Gaines was assigned as a research analyst through the Oakridge Institute for Science and Education (ORISE) fellowship program. Prior to her work with the FBI, she was employed as a police officer for the City of Richmond in Virginia. She is currently working on her PsyD and has conducted numerous psychological assessments, intake evaluations, individual and group psychotherapy, as well as, crisis counseling. As a research analyst, she provides analytical support for crimes against adults research projects. These projects include serial murder, sexual homicide, serial rape, sexual sadism, high level white collar offenders, and campus attackers.

Lightning Source UK Ltd.
Milton Keynes UK
UKHW051642241120
373997UK00003B/16